UNDERSTANDING WATCHMAN NEE

Dana Roberts

The Newest Book on Watchman Nee

UNDERSTANDING WATCHMAN NEE

haven books
Division of Logos International
Plainfield, N.J. 07060

UNDERSTANDING WATCHMAN NEE
Copyright © 1980 by Logos International
All rights reserved
Printed in the United States of America
Library of Congress Number: 80-83839
International Standard Book Number: 0-88270-489-3
Logos International, Plainfield, New Jersey 07060

Contents

Preface

My own acquaintance with Watchman Nee's writing began in 1967, at a time before his name became prominent in America's search for spiritual values. I was an adolescent physically and spiritually a babe, and I at least wanted to get beyond the "proof-text-flip" or three-chapters-a-night Bible routine. I sought counsel among those I judged spiritually mature. My pastor enthusiastically recommended Nee's *The Normal Christian Life.* "Strangely warmed" by the lucidity with which Nee interpreted Romans, I thereupon read *The Spiritual Man* and realized that here was a real dynamo of spiritual imagination that would drive many a church to reconsider its values.

As more publications followed, my enthusiasm persisted, to the degree that I have undertaken extensive research into his life and teachings. What five years uncovered was not necessarily flattering and has made me somewhat suspicious of unsubstantiated accounts of religious folk heroes. This book represents part of my research and analysis. I hope it will answer some of the questions and penetrate some of the mystique surrounding Watchman Nee as a teacher and theologian.

This study was accomplished through the aid of other brothers in Christ to whom thanks are gratefully given here. First to Dr. Harvey J.S. Blaney, who first encouraged me to write a master's dissertation on Nee. Warmest thanks are given to the faculty of Eastern Nazarene College, especially Drs. Wilbur H. Mullen, Albert L. Truesdale and Alvin H. Kauffman for guiding me in the preparation of this book. In addition I would like to thank those who advised me in my research: The Rev. Edwin Stube; Drs. Douglas Stuart and Roger R. Nicole, librarian Robert Dvorak and his associate, Kenneth Umenhofer, all from the faculty of Gordon-Conwell Theological Seminary; Rev. W.H. Holton of the Alliance Bible Seminary on Cheung Chaus Island, Hong Kong; Dr. Charles W. Carter of the China Evangelical Seminary in Taipei, Taiwan; and Dr. A. Donald Fredlund of Christian Literature Crusade. I would also like to thank Mr. Wing-Tai Leung and Miss Joyce Leung for translating and making available to me certain Chinese sources. And lastly I wish to thank my wife, Cindy, for her patience during the writing of this book.

On June 1, 1972, in a prison camp in Anhwei Province, China, Watchman Nee, one of the most popular contemporary theologians,* died from natural causes. A man of immense ability as a preacher and writer, his ministry was not hindered during his twenty-year incarceration for being an apolitical and independent religious leader. No longer in the position to preach openly, his messages were published before his death in over thirty volumes in many languages. Through the printed media his books continue to influence the interpretation of the Bible within the global evangelical movement.

In America during the same twenty-year period the phenomenon of renewal within the church has manifested itself in at least three different movements: the prayer group, the charismatic movement, and the Jesus People Movement. To some extent the writings of Watchman Nee have been influential in all three.

Beginning in the early 1960s small unstructured prayer groups developed out of a desire on the part of many church members to meet personal needs, to participate

---

*By 1975 *The Normal Christian Life* alone had been published into more than 440,000 copies in the American edition. A. Donald Fredlund, Publications Secretary, Christian Literature Crusade, personal letter, February 24, 1975.

and express themselves in the church, to meet other members and to attain a clear walk with God/Christ. A prayer group usually involved a time of sharing, prayer and the study of the Bible and/or a Christian book. Many of these groups began studying Nee's books, particularly *The Normal Christian Life, The Release of the Spirit, What Shall This Man Do?* and *The Normal Christian Worker.* A common sentiment among many prayer groups was the view that in some way the work and the power of the Holy Spirit had abated in the church since the apostolic age. Through the study of books like John Sherrills's *They Speak with Other Tongues* a part of the prayer group renewal was channeled into the charismatic movement.

The charismatic movement, the largest of the renewal movements, has involved members of all Christian faiths, including Roman Catholic and Orthodox churches. Books dealing with the history of the movement give three significant inceptions: the ministry of Pentecostal minister David J. du Plessis in traditional churches and organizations, the work of the Full Gospel Business Men's Fellowship, and the Reverend Dennis Bennett's confession of speaking in tongues before his Episcopal congregation in Van Nuys, California, on April 3, 1960.[1]

The movement's primary characteristic has been a renewed interest in the charisms described in the Book of Acts and First Corinthians, chapters 12-14. The individual reception of these gifts is believed to occur after an initial outpouring of the Spirit upon the believer called the baptism in the Holy Spirit. While remaining within the rich theological traditions of Protestantism and Roman

Catholicism, charismatics have drawn their ideas from writers of varying traditions. Apart from theologians within the movement itself, one of the most widely read theologians is Watchman Nee.

Nee's books have provided many charismatics with a theological basis to call in question or reject many of the ecstatic outbursts that seemed to hinder the church's primary responsibility to preach Christ. Reading his books on theological anthropology, many Pentecostals and charismatic church leaders became convinced that not all tongue speaking nor all prophecy have their origin in the Holy Spirit. Nor does the presence of true *charismata* necessarily indicate a person's moral integrity.

His books on ecclesiology have provided many with a theological bridge between the structured organization of the denomination and the more spontaneous form of Pentecostal worship. Through *Spiritual Authority, What Shall This Man Do?* and his works on the life of the church, many charismatics were able to find a comfortable balance between diocesan (district) authority and the Pentecostal tendency toward more lay leadership and participation.

The latest movement, the Jesus People, originated from the missionary activities of a number of conservative evangelists.[2] Recognizing that the youth of the counter-culture were not to be enamored with what they called "middle-class churchianity"* of the liberal or legalistically

---

*The term is used to designate all of the characteristics of the denominations that were rejected. The Jesus People are particularly offended with the church's lack of emphasis on Christ as the source of salvation, the importance of conversion and recognition of the church as the eschatological

fundamental churches, these ministers preached a new message on a "street level" that would appeal to youth's desire for spiritual revelation, a sense of communal love and a need for personal involvement with a cause. Within a few years the Jesus People had become a global phenomenon.

Although the movement contains conservative and radical factions, certain beliefs are generally held in common. Salvation is not found on the basis of intellectual assent to church doctrine, nor on church membership, but on a conversion experience and on a continuing personal relationship with God through Christ. Christ's "great commission" to the church is largely carried out through street witnessing, bumper stickers, Jesus marches and "Jesus Is the Rock" concerts, in a manner most appealing to their own peer groups. Most Jesus People blame the institutionalization of worship and the acceptance of false doctrines as the cause of the church's ills. Their solution is to establish a community of believers led by the Holy Spirit. More radical groups, such as the Children of God, accept an imminent premillennial return of Christ requiring drastic methods of evangelism. With the exception of their own newspapers and tracts, the most popular books are Nee's *The Normal*

---

community. Socially, they would also agree with Pierre Berton's assessment in *The Comfortable Pew:*

> The worship of conformity and respectability, which distinguishes the religious establishment, turns religion and Christianity into separate entities. Religion, the cult of the establishment, with its denial of Christian radicalism, its alliance with the status quo and its awesome social power, is, indeed, often the antithesis of Christianity. ([Philadelphia and New York: J.B. Lippincott Co. 1965], p. 68)

Christian Life, The Normal Christian Church Life and, among the more ascetic, world-abandoning groups, his *Love Not the World.*

Even the charismatic Indonesian Revival of the 1970s had been affected by Nee's teachings. Although only *The Normal Christian Life* has been published in Malay, the state language, evangelical missionaries carried his writings with them. The Reverend Edwin Stube, an Episcopal missionary to Indonesia, established many congregations on the basis of Nee's eldership concept and instruction on the spiritual life:

> . . . I got hold of *The Normal New Testament Church Life [sic]* this revolutionized my thinking about the New Testament order in the church. We have been trying to apply all these principles in our fellowship here and in the congregations we founded in the villages. Other books which have helped our understanding of certain aspects of the Christian life have been *Sit, Walk, Stand, Changed into His Likeness,* and most deep of all the commentary *Song of Songs.* At one point in the life of our community here we began to receive much new light on God's present purpose in the church particularly in the formation of a people for end-time ministry. Then we got a copy of *The Glorious Church* and were surprised to see that he had been teaching all the exact same things 30 years ago.[3]

An increased interest in biblical and theological sources of faith, a reemphasis on lay participation and leadership, and the experiencing of charismatic authority all contributed to Nee's current notoriety. But the primary reason for his popularity among all renewal groups was his "understanding of spiritual things." As Ellis Larson has shown, the primary emphasis of the church renewal groups was the dynamics of the Spirit.[4] These dynamics have as their focal point the concept of a spiritual reality, which many have discovered through the works of Watchman Nee.

Having experienced a direct, personal, religious experience in conversion, many of them found the writings of contemporary theologians inadequate, too complicated or spurious, in their opinion. The works of Paul Tillich, Karl Barth and Søren Kierkegaard appealed to individuals far more theoretical or intellectual than the general populace of the church. On the other hand, Nee's books were meaningful to those involved with a personal encounter with Christ, regardless of their capacity to read sophisticated theology.

Nee's words also revived among many evangelicals a feeling that the meaning and message of the Bible was far more profound than any other classical work of literature. This view is inherent in Nee's conception of the Bible, which he asserted to be in accord with all true knowledge of God:

> If a person is not regenerated, then no matter how clever and scholarly he may be, to him this book is a mystery. But a regenerated man whose cultural background may be quite primitive possesses greater understanding of the Bible than does an unregenerated college professor. And the explanation? One of them has a regenerated spirit, while the other has not. The Scriptures cannot be mastered through cleverness, research, or natural talent. The word of God is spirit, therefore it can only be known

to whoever possesses a regenerated spirit. Since the root
and the nature of the Bible are spiritual, how can anyone
who lacks a regenerated spirit begin to understand it? It is
a closed book to him.[5]

While this idea is one of the finer points of his writings, it
is also the most vulnerable to criticism for establishing a
form of gnosticism and fostering spiritual pride.

The Scope of This Study

As a pathfinder in the modern church's quest for
lasting spiritual renewal, it is important to begin to
question Nee's qualifications and his choice of methods.
What training and life experiences have prepared him to
lead others on the way to spiritual maturity? Is the Bible,
inspired by the Holy Spirit, the sole compass of his faith?
Or has some less accurate device detoured him from the
Christian "walk in newness of life" (Rom. 6:4)?

The aim of this book is to answer these and other
questions and to provide a thorough survey and analysis
of his life and thought. The first chapter deals with his
life and ministry. Besides providing an overview of Nee's
life and that of the "Little Flock,"* a reconstruction of the
theological roots of Nee's beliefs according to his Christian
education will be given. Sources for this biography
include Nee's own testimony, historical sources and
secondary biographies. The chapter will conclude with a
history of the Little Flock under the influence of Nee's
co-worker and chief exponent, Witness Lee.

Chapter two is a brief description of Nee's voluminous

---

*The churches founded by Nee and his co-workers are hesitant to label their
movement as a whole. Outsiders have given them this term from *The Little
Flock Hymnal* which they published and used in their services.

works and presents a historical, textual and stylistic appraisal upon which to evaluate the content of Nee's theology. The next three chapters serve as the core of this thesis and analyze Nee's theology in three areas: the Word of God, anthropology and ecclesiology. This book ends with a summary of the evidence and a conclusion.

UNDERSTANDING WATCHMAN NEE

Watchman Nee and the Work of the Little Flock

In the century before 1949 the nation of China underwent two cultural revolutions. The first, brought about by European commercial and imperial interests, resulted in a cultural shift from Oriental custom to Occidental tradition in matters of government, technology and social structure. The second, concurrent in time and location with the first, established Christianity as a numerically significant religion in China. In essence the historical and cultural setting of Watchman Nee's career and teachings are reflective of the conflict and harmony existing in the Oriental, Occidental and Christian cultures.

Parents and Native Residence

On October 19, 1899, Nee Wen-Hsiu of Foochow, a maritime customs officer serving in Swatow, married Lin Ho-P'ing, the adopted daughter of a wealthy businessman. Although the service was performed in a Christian (Anglican) church in Nan-t'ai, the marriage had been arranged according to Oriental custom, and the conjugal celebrants had not met before the day of their wedding.

Wen-Hsiu's father, Nee U-Cheng, was a congregational minister affiliated with the American Board of Missions, headquartered in the district capitol of

Foochow.* As a result of the Treaty of Nanking (1842) that ended the Opium War, Foochow had become one of the first successful Protestant missionary centers in China. Under the terms of the treaty, Great Britain and China both agreed to protect trading and missionary posts in the five ports of Canton, Amoy, Shanghai, Ningpo and Foochow. Missions were quickly established in Foochow, first by the Boston-based American Board, followed shortly by the Anglicans and the Episcopal Methodists. But the religious victories won in the Nanking Treaty became a hindrance to effective evangelism. Missionaries came to rely too heavily on the military arm of the British Consulate,† and the local population began associating Christianity with "imperialism." This particularly affected the Anglican missions, whom the people associated with the British opium trade.‡

Nevertheless in 1853 Nga U-Cheng, Watchman Nee's grandfather, was won over to the Christian message. He then began attending the American Board's school established outside of Foochow. Records of the Foochow mission show a prescribed number of books in the school's

------

*Located twenty-five miles upstream from the mouth of the river Minchiang, Foochow is a commercial city that is known for its tea and orange trade. In 1920 its population exceeded 624,000.[1]

†Prime Minister Lord Salisbury at the bicentennial meeting of the Society for the Propagation of the Gospel (1900) said, "But now if a Boniface or a Columba [names of churches] is exposed to these martyrdoms, the result is an appeal to the consul and the mission of a gunboat. . . . I must not conceal from you that at the Foreign Office the missionaries are not popular."[2]

‡"I weep over the melancholy fact, but I cannot wonder at it whoever else may do so: for our Chinese missionaries have all along been counteracted by the influence of the opium trade."[3] Chinese anti-Christian literature assumed that native converts had been given a thought-controlling pill.[4]

required curriculum. Included among these was John L. Nevius's three-volume theology, *Compendium of Theology.* As a missionary to China himself, Nevius (1829-93) offered the Chinese an explanation for the apparent diversity of ethics among self-professed (Western) Christians. Sanctification, he argued, involved "a psychological battle between soul and spirit."[5] Therefore new Christians should understand that not all believers live according to the spirit.

By 1857 U-Cheng had learned his lesson well enough to become a baptized member. Recognized by his Occidental superiors as a natural preacher, he became the second ordained Chinese minister of the congregational mission in Fukien Province on June 4, 1876.[6] Having a large family, he was given a salary of eleven dollars a month, by nineteenth-century Chinese standards a substantial sum of money. One year later, his fourth son, Wen-Hsiu, was born.

A few days after his father's death (1890) Wen-Hsiu took the three-day-long Confucian competitive examinations. These exams were a test of classical skills in literature, which the imperial government used to determine who could best serve in civil positions as a representative of Chinese tradition. Wen-Hsiu was awarded the second-degree level, ensuring him a job in the government the rest of his life.

The life of Ho-P'ing, his wife and Watchman Nee's mother, had been far more difficult. A strong influence on her son's personal and spiritual development, her life was expressive of the cross-cultural shift so characteristic of the period of China's greatest church growth. Born into a large non-Christian family during the famine of 1880, she was sold by her father to a family that was better off.* She was again sold to a merchant named Lin of Nan-ta'i. Although the merchant loved children, he adhered to the aesthetic tradition of foot binding.†

The same year as Ho-P'ing's adoption, Mr. Lin became seriously ill with a mysterious disease that was undiagnosable and untreatable by both Chinese and Western doctors. Upon the recommendation of one of Lin's business associates, they sought out the aid of a Methodist pastor who believed in healing. A dramatic recovery followed. Just as dramatic was the change in the Lin household. The family idols were discarded. Mr. Lin and his wife were baptized into the Methodist church. Ho-P'ing's painful foot binding ended, and she, according to her own testimony, rejoiced in the hymns and Bible stories taught her.

Like most Christians her new life was not always harmonious with her consecration. While attending the Chinese Western Girls School in Shanghai in preparation for an American medical school education, Ho-P'ing became involved in worldly interests and pleasures. In her autobiography, *An Object of Grace and Love*, she writes, "I learned there much of the pride of life and some of the sins of the flesh."[7] Once moved by the faith of a young visiting missionary, Miss Dora Yu, she was still unwilling

---

*Some of Ho-P'ing's peers fared much worse. Infanticide was a common practice. (See footnote 8.)

†In this procedure each foot was bound tightly so that the yet unossified heel and tarsus were forced together. Each day the binding was tightened further in a manner that ensured continuous pain until she reached physical maturity. The idea was to produce "lily feet" that could fit into a teacup.

to give up her interests. Her weakness for worldly things would again reveal itself years after her marriage.

Completing her English studies in Shanghai, her plans to travel to America met with disappointment. Her mother opposed her trip and permanently delayed it by arranging a marriage for her adopted daughter with the son of the late Pastor Nga (Nee in Fukien dialect). She was bound by custom, for no Fukien girl had ever broken a marriage arrangement.

Birth and Early Education

Four years after her marriage Nee Ho-P'ing was in distress with the expectancy of her third child. Her first two both had been girls, a personal disgrace to her responsibilities as a bearer of the male heir. Her mother-in-law feared she would be like the wife of her eldest son, who bore six children, all females. In her anguish Ho-P'ing promised that if the Lord gave her a boy, she would return him back for His service.

On November 4, 1903, in Swatow, a male child, Nee Shu-Tsu, was born. His name means "he who proclaims his ancestors' merits." Years later, after the boy's mission in life became more evident, she proposed a new name, To-Sheng, "the sound of a gong." The name would remind both mother and son that he would be a "bell ringer" (or Watchman) who would raise the people of God for service.

Shortly thereafter the Nee family returned to their ancestral home of Foochow. There Watchman began his education in both classical and Christian studies. A tutor appointed by the elder Nee instructed him in calligraphy, the ethical maxims contained in the traditional Four Books and Five Classics, and the Chinese musical system called The Melodies. In hand with this Oriental instruction, his mother taught him Christian hymns and Bible lessons. In all Nee showed intellectual promise.

But by 1912 it became apparent that a classical tradition was no longer as important as it once had been in attaining vocational success. The two hundred sixty-eight-year, archaic Manchu Dynasty had been overthrown, and Sun Yat-Sen's *Kuomintang* appeared to be gaining the support of a majority of the people. With its slogans of "Love One's Country" and "Nationalism, Democracy and Livelihood," the movement popularized the benefits of Western culture, including its educational values. The long, plaited queues were cut off, and Western educational institutions benefited with increased enrollment.

In the Nee household Sun Yat-Sen became the family hero. As an advocate of women's rights, Sun was particularly appealing to Nee's mother. Through her lectures and correspondence Ho-P'ing founded the local Women's Patriotic Society. While her husband was less enthusiastic, he desired that Watchman should receive a Western-Christian education. He sent Nee to three schools: The Church Missionary Society's vernacular school, St. Mark's High School (English) and, finally, Trinity College.

Trinity College, Foochow, had been founded by W.S. Packenham-Walsh, a former student of the Anglican Trinity College in Dublin, Ireland. Commissioned by the Church Missionary Society, he went to Fukien with the sincere hope of preaching Christ and ridding the com-

munity there of such habits as foot binding, infanticide*
and the custom of some widows of hanging themselves
publicly to be reunited with their departed husbands.
Nevertheless, he was a product of the Victorian Age and
never permitted his English dignity to be relaxed so that
all men might hear his message. Wherever he went he
always wanted a tablecloth on his eating table as a mark
of civilization. Once when he was crossing a river he had
permitted some people to ride in the boat with him. But
when one of his fellow passengers boarded a flock of
goats, he later wrote, "This I felt was exceedingly the
limits even of Christian toleration, so I had them all
turned out . . ."[10]

His missionary efforts met with greater success when
he offered the Chinese something they desired, a quality
education. By 1905 he had purchased the property of the
former Russian Consulate on the Black Stone Hill in Foochow and established a junior college there. He named it
in honor of his alma mater and staffed it with Dublin
professors. The school instructed and preached the gospel
by interpreting Chinese classics in the light of the Bible.
The Word was also ministered through Anglican matins
given in Chinese.

Nee found the school's paramilitary form of discipline
with its "Western" form of worship not to his liking. In a
testimony given some fifteen years after leaving college,
Nee reflected on his attitude toward Christianity and
preaching at that time:

---

*Near the school a baby tower had been constructed to provide a burial place
for the children of the poor. Like the trash and dung heaps of the Roman
Empire,[8] it became the place to discard unwanted children.[9]

Formerly I had despised preachers and preaching because in those days most preachers were the employees of European or American missionaries, having to be servile to them, and earning merely eight or nine dollars each month. I had never imagined for a moment that I would become a preacher, a profession which I regarded as trifling and base.[11]

While some students were converted by the Church of England propers given in the chapel services, Nee clearly sided with many of the senior students who demonstrated a proclivity to antireligious sentiments.

His dissatisfaction with Christianity affirmed itself in his academic activities. An excellent student in all subjects except the Bible, Nee preferred to read cheap novels that were smuggled into the school rather than to labor over the Scripture. Consequently, to save face with his Christian parents, he resorted to cheating in order to pass his Bible exams.

Conversion

Concurrent with this time Nee's mother had received a place of honor for her political activities. Society ladies began coming to her house and introduced her to the pursuits of the elite: playing cards and mah-jong. Thereafter her interests turned away from religion and politics to social pleasure.

Her lapse of faith became evident to Watchman when in January of 1920 she wrongly accused him of breaking a valuable ornament. Though he refused to confess, she gave him a thrashing. Later she discovered his innocence in the matter, but she was without remorse, and according to tradition did not admit her error to her son out of pride of her position in the family.*

A month later Miss Dora Yu, the woman evangelist who had impressed Ho-P'ing earlier, began revival meetings in the Methodist Tien-An Chapel.[12] In respect of their former association, Ho-P'ing attended the first services. Convicted by the Holy Spirit she soon told her gambling friends, "I am a Christian, Miss Yu has come a long distance to preach here . . . I shall not play tomorrow!"[13] She later became a well-known Methodist preacher, whose speaking tours included her native China and Malaya.

Under the strong conviction of her sins she tearfully went to Watchman to seek forgiveness. Before her husband and her children, she threw her arms around him and cried, "For the Lord Jesus' sake, I confess to beating you unjustly and in anger."[14] He at first seemed little moved by her confession, but that same night he also became a convert to Christ:

> On the evening of 29th April, 1920, I was alone in my room, struggling to decide whether or not to believe in the Lord. At first I was reluctant but as I tried to pray I saw the magnitude of my sins and the reality and efficacy of Jesus as the Savior. As I visualized the Lord's hands stretched out on the cross, they seemed to be welcoming me and the Lord was saying, "I am waiting here to receive you." Realizing the effectiveness of Christ's blood in cleansing my sins and being overwhelmed by such love, I accepted him there. Previously I had laughed at people who had

---

*In the Confucian tradition the instruction of filial piety requires that a parent should never submit to her children.

accepted Jesus, but that evening the experience became real for me and I wept and confessed my sins, seeking the Lord's forgiveness. As I made my first prayer I knew joy and peace such as I had never known before. Light seemed to flood the room and I said to the Lord, "Oh Lord, you have indeed been gracious to me."[15]

The next day he attended one of Miss Yu's meetings and openly proclaimed his salvation by going forward.

Stimulated perhaps by his mother's example, Nee believed that "Christian repentance includes the confession of past faults,"[16] in addition to a change of conduct. He no longer cheated in his Bible tests, and he openly confessed to the school principal that he had written the answers to tests on his palms. The normal procedure for this type of rule infraction was expulsion. Because of his honesty, however, the principal declined to dismiss him. Except for a one-year absence in which he attended Miss Yu's Bible school in Shanghai, Nee continued his studies at Trinity, vigorously witnessing to his friends and fellow students.

Theological Education

Discarding much of his theological training at Trinity, a majority of Nee's teachings and exegetical methods are traceable to instruction received apart from his formal schooling. Two Bible schools, extensive theological reading, and a methodical study of the Bible subsequent to his college education are responsible for much of the depth of his teaching.

During the 1920-21 school period he stayed at Miss Yu's Bible school in Shanghai. From her he learned to let the Holy Spirit speak to his own heart through God's Word. Memorizing Scripture texts was important, but one had to permit the Scripture to be an instrument of God's will through revelation. Miss Yu also taught him to trust in the Lord for his needs and not to be concerned with worldly pursuits. This instruction proved to be a difficult message for him and was one of the reasons that led him to seek a "second blessing." In his own testimony he admitted to being a "fleshly or carnal believer"* and to the irreconcilability of his actions and the school's discipline:

> Before very long she politely expelled me from the institute with the explanation that it was inconvenient for me to stay any longer. Because of my gourmet appetite, dilettante dress and tardy arising in the mornings Sister Yu thought fit to send me home. My desire to serve the Lord had been dealt a serious blow. Although I thought my life had been transformed, in fact there remained many more things to be changed.[18]

Even though Nee had seen some fruit, he was not satisfied with his Christian growth:

> Though some people had been saved I was not satisfied, since many in the school and in the town were unaffected, and I felt the need to be filled with the Holy Spirit and to receive power from above.[19]

At Dora Yu's suggestion he went to Miss M.E. Barber, a British missionary. She instructed him in the Keswick

---

*This is the term used by Nee for those Christians who are dominated by some natural necessity of the human body (nourishment, reproduction and defense).[17]

concept of the victorious life through the filling of the Holy Spirit.

> I returned to school to seek the filling of the Holy Spirit and the love of Christ, but I found that I still could not say with conviction the words of the Psalm [Ps. 73:25]. At last on February 13th, 1922 I was willing to lay aside this relationship [with Chang Pin-huei (Charity), his future wife, who at this time was not a Christian] and then I knew an experience of great elation. On the day I was converted I shook off the burden of my sins, but on this later occasion my heart was emptied of everything that would separate me from God. From then on people began to be saved. On that day I changed my fine clothes for a simple garment, went into the kitchen, made some paste, and with a bundle of gospel posters on my arm, went out into the street to post them on the walls and to distribute gospel tracts. In those days in Foochow, Fukien Province, this was a pioneer act. From the second term of 1922, I prayed daily for those school friends whose names were in my notebook, and many of them were saved.[20]

During the first seven years following his "baptism in the Holy Spirit," Nee's ministry rapidly expanded. As a result of the revival at Trinity College, Nee received the assistance of a number of co-workers in his ministry to the school and the surrounding towns and provinces. In 1923 he began the publication of religious materials, including the magazine *The Present Testimony,* and went on numerous speaking tours, practices which continued to be a part of his ministry until his arrest during Mao Tse-tung's "Cultural Revolution." The relative success of the work caused Nee to conclude that his movement had a relatively clear "understanding of the gospel of grace."[21] But he desired to further clarify in his own mind the distinction between grace and law; the kingdom of heaven and eternal life; grace and reward; and salvation and victory.[22] At the suggestion of Dora Yu, Nee sought the instruction of a teacher more mature than himself in the ways of the Lord, Miss Margaret E. Barber.

Like Nee, Miss Barber had become disenchanted with Anglican doctrine and polity. In 1909 while on furlough from her missionary post at the Nan-t'ai girls' middle school, she began to seriously question the church's position on infant baptism. To the dismay of her bishop she began attending the services at the independent Surrey Chapel, Norwich. Under the teaching of Rev. David M. Panton, she adjudged baptism to be actually a baptism into the Lord's death. In this death they believed that the believer separated himself from the "world" and its perdition.[23] Just as Christ's death concluded with the resurrection unto life, so also the believer received resurrection into the church with newness of life.*

In 1920 after severing her ties with the Anglican Church Missionary Society, she returned to China as an independent missionary under the sponsorship of Surrey Chapel. In short time she was joined by her friend Miss L.S. Ballord and an independent Chinese woman preacher, Li Ai-ming. Feeling that God was calling them to train natives for church leadership, they rented a twenty-room building to serve as a school. In a manner testifying to this witness, Watchman Nee and many who had become

---

*"The Fourfold Work of the Cross" in chapter 4.

Christians through his and Miss Yu's ministry* attended her classes and personal instruction on the spiritual life.

No single person is more responsible for the development of Nee's theology than Miss Barber. While he later rejected her teaching ministry to men as inappropriate to the woman's responsibility in the church, he repeatedly acknowledged her influence as a "light" in his own life.[25] Despite this difference of opinion, he continued to seek her advice and counsel until shortly before her death in May 1930. As evidence of her own affection for him, Miss Barber designated in her will that he receive her most prized possession, her Bible.

A devoted reader, Nee took advantage of Miss Barber's library. There he availed himself of much of the holiness literature influential in Great Britain as a result of the Keswick Movement and the Welsh Revival.[26] Their significance in his own studies is corroborated by his frequent references to such holiness writers as Andrew Murray, Evan Roberts, T. Austin Sparks and Jessie Penn-Lewis. Some of these books even provided the essential outline of thought to his own books. Mrs. Jessie Penn-Lewis (1861-1927), the Welsh teacher and evangelist, set the tone for the spiritual and anthropological emphasis of Nee's writings.†

---

*One student, Leland Wang, founded the China Overseas Missionary Union in Indonesia and continues to be active in a Hong Kong church.[24]

†Raised in a Calvinistic Methodist home in Wales, Jessie Penn-Lewis suffered from a chronic, debilitating lung ailment throughout her life. After her marriage to an accountant she began attending services at Holy Trinity Church in Richmond, Surrey. The pastor, the Reverend Evan H. Hopkins, a leading theologian of the early Keswick Conventions, preached victory over sins through the cross of Christ, full surrender to Him, and an enduement

14

A feature of all of Mrs. Penn-Lewis' literature is the theme of "spiritual warfare" among the parts of man's nature. In her books on the cross, the "flesh" must be crucified so that the human spirit, the "god-consciousness" of man, is active.[27] The "I" of the old creation must be yielded to the cross, so that man, no longer loving his "soul"—the "self-consciousness"—can walk "not after the flesh, but after the spirit."[28] Once the human spirit has been released from the bondage of the soul, it may be open to the Holy Spirit's leading.

The high regard that both Watchman Nee and M.E. Barber shared for this Welsh lady is brought to light in this narrative taken from Angus Kinnear's biography:

> He asked Miss Barber if she could not lend him something to read on the subject of the cross. Yes, she said, she had two books, but she would not give them to him at present; she would rather wait until he was mature enough to read them. "I could not understand the reason for this," he says, "and I wanted those two books very much, so I obtained them by guile. I inquired from her the titles and author without her realizing what I was doing,

---

with power for service subsequent to conversion. In complete accord with this Keswick theology, she later became a lecturer and author on the "abundant life." When the Welsh Revival started in 1902 she had wholly supported it as "the rushing mighty breath upon the land." But when religious enthusiasm turned into uncontrolled ecstasy, Mrs. Penn-Lewis, together with Evan Roberts, became one of its most well-known critics. After the revival she considered it her particular ministry to set up "consultative conferences" to instruct believers about the spiritual warfare and the work of Satan in counterfeiting spiritual reality. Her battle plans for this psychic war and anthropological struggle dominated the three booklets she wrote during this period (*War on the Saints, The Spiritual Warfare* and *Soul and Spirit*). Her last book's emphasis on dividing of soul and spirit according to Heb. 4:12 reinforced the formulation of Nee's theology.

and I wrote off to Mrs. Penn-Lewis, who sent them to me
as a gift and wrote me a nice letter as well! One was
The Word of the Cross and the other *The Cross and Its
Message.* Well, I read them most carefully, but though I
received help of a kind, to my disappointment they didn't
settle my biggest question. That, I find, is not God's way,
to give us quick answers."[29]

Both Barber and Nee subscribed to her magazine, *The
Overcomer,** which permitted them to become familiar
with Andrew Murray, F.B. Meyer, Madame Guyon and
George Müller.

With some reservation Miss Barber lent him her
Plymouth Brethren collection of expository writings by
C.A. Coates and J. Nelson Darby. Much pleased by their
sense of revelation he wrote to Mr. George Ware, a
London publisher, and received copies of books by C.H.
Mackintosh *(Notes on the Pentateuch),* William Kelly,
Charles Stanley and George Cutting, whose booklet
"Safety, Certainty, and Enjoyment" was a favorite of
Nee's. In 1945 in a series of messages Nee summarized
the influence of the Brethren upon his thought and that
of the churches he founded:

They showed us how the blood of the Lord satisfies the
righteousness of God; the assurance of salvation; how the
weakest believer may be accepted in Christ, just as Christ
was accepted; how to believe in the Word of God as the

---

*The magazine was founded in 1909 and continues to be published by the
Overcomer Literature Trust. The single emphasis on teaching faith is evident
in the issues printed during World War II. The only reference to the war was
an obituary about one of the magazine's secretaries who was killed during an
air raid.

foundation of salvation. Since church history began, there never was a period when the gospel was clearer than in that time. Not only so, it was also they who showed us that the church cannot gain the entire world, that the church has a heavenly calling, and that the church has no worldly hope. It was they who also opened up prophecies for the first time, causing us to see that the return of the Lord is the hope of the church. It was they who opened the Book of Revelation and the Book of Daniel and showed us the kingdom, the tribulation, the rapture, and the bride. Without them, we would have known today a very small percentage of future things. It was also they who showed us what the law of sin is, what it is to be set free, what it is to be crucified with Christ, what it is to be raised with Christ, how to be identified with the Lord through faith, and how to be transformed daily by looking unto Him. It was they who showed us the sin of denominations, the unity of the Body of Christ, and the unity of the Holy Spirit. It was they who showed us the difference between Judaism and the Church. In the Roman Catholic Church and the Protestant churches, this difference could not be readily seen, but they made us see it anew. It was also they who showed us the sin of the mediatorial class, how all the children of God are priests, and how all can serve God. It was they who recovered for us the principle of meetings in I Corinthians 14, showing us that prophesying is not based upon ordination, but upon the gift of the Holy Spirit. If we were to enumerate one by one what they recovered, we may as well say that in today's pure Protestant churches there is not one truth that they had recovered or recovered more.[30]

As his work expanded, Nee endeavored to keep a soundly scriptural basis for his theology and to preserve

himself within the historic "witness of the Spirit" within
the church. In studying the Bible he supplemented his
own insights with that of C.I. Scofield, Robert Young,
Samuel P. Tregelles, F.W. Grant, Henry Alford, B.F.
Westcott and J.B. Lightfoot.

Beyond Brethren and Keswick materials Nee read and
studied the lives of such diverse church figures as Hudson
Taylor, John Bunyon, A.B. Simpson, Sadhu Sundar Singh,
Dwight L. Moody, Charles G. Finney, C.H. Spurgeon,
John Wesley, Jonathan Edwards, David Brainerd, Martin
Luther, John Knox, George Whitefield and Cardinal John
Henry Newman.

Development of the Little Flock

Nee's legacy to the contemporary church is not limited
to his voluminous writings. While there has been a large
number of Christian writers in the two millennia of the
church, Nee shares with a much smaller group the distinction of being a founder of a sect within Christendom.
Dividing himself from other denominations quite early
in the Christian life, his church began in a much more
auspicious way than the Methodist or Lutheran Church.

One of Miss Yu's students, Leland Wang (Wang Tsai),
had a room large enough to serve as a place for believers
and students to come together for prayer and Bible study.
In 1922 Wang, his wife, Watchman and his mother began
to meet there. As is the custom of such informal meetings,
each shared a testimony of what God was doing in his or
her life and prayed for the particular needs of the group
or for the needs of others. While none of them were
official clergy, they felt the real need to "show the Lord's

death"[31] by sharing the Lord's Supper. Through this lay worship they had a real sense of "joy and release" that communicated itself to others, and in a few weeks they were joined by others.

Like Charles Wesley's "Holy Club" at Oxford they felt a real responsibility to the community and actively campaigned for the Lord through religious processions and evangelistic rallies. They adopted the custom of wearing "gospel shirts"—long white cotton sheets which carried short Bible verses in large Chinese characters: "Repent and believe the gospel"; "God so loved the world." Beating drums and singing hymns as they went, they would gather large crowds into rented halls to hear their message or that of Miss Ruth Lee, a converted atheist.

For three years this type of ministry continued. But problems arose between Leland Wang, the real head of the group, and Watchman Nee. Despite the efforts of Miss Barber to heal the relationship, Nee was reluctant to submit to the decisions of Wang that he considered unscriptural.

Ironically, the disagreement was over the unity of the church. Nee contended that their ministry should not just emotionally stir up the people, but they should work to form new churches that would minister continually a life-giving message. In his characteristic style he described how he discovered his error through an inner, anthropological revelation:

> I had to admit that even when I was right by human standards, the inner life pronounced me wrong. . . . From that day I began to see more and more clearly that in relation to any course of action, even if others pronounced

it right, and I myself considered it right, and every aspect of the case indicated that it was right, I must still be very sensitive to the reactions of the life of Christ within me. As we advance in the approved course, does the inner life grow stronger or weaker? Does the inner "anointing" confirm the rightness of the course, or does an absence of the "anointing" indicate that the divine approval is withheld? God's way for us is not known by external indications but by internal registrations. It is peace and joy in the spirit that indicate the Christian's path.[32]

In 1925 on the suggestion of Wang, Nee went with his mother to Sitiawan, Malaya, for a speaking tour. Their meetings there met with some success, despite the fact that most of the natives were more interested in tapping rubber trees than in "touching spiritual reality."[33] It did give him time to pray for direction, and upon his return to China he formally broke from the Foochow group and established his headquarters in the neighborhood of Pagoda.

During his ministry at Pagoda Nee made a number of trips to the areas of Amoy, Julongsu, Changchow and Tungan. Speaking to large groups within and outside of traditional churches, Nee would take down the names of those who responded to his messages and send them copies of his *Revival Magazine*.

At one visit to the Talmadge College and Seminary of the American Presbyterian Mission, Nee met his old associate Ruth Lee. She was working with the Spiritual Light Publishing Society and persuaded him to work there also. For a few months he worked faithfully for them in Nanking, but his own attitude towards Western missions would reaffirm itself as a result of a strain in Christian-pagan relations.

Like a returning nightmare antimissionary riots broke out in Foochow and Shanghai, and the death of Sun Yat-sen made the fate of international groups uncertain. While some semblance of civil order was restored under the Commander-in-Chief of the Army, Chiang Kai-shek, Nee was determined to form a new church totally non-Western and based upon the concept of one church for one locality.

Not long after, however, serious illness would temporarily postpone his preaching plans, giving him, however, an opportunity to prepare his messages. In Shanghai a doctor told him that he had a serious, if not fatal, case of tuberculosis and that he needed rest and good nourishment. Returning to Pagoda Anchorage, he spent the next four months rapidly deteriorating, despite the care provided for him by Miss Barber and the students at her school. "For two months, I lived daily in the very jaws of Satan," he wrote.[34] Nevertheless his condition improved at the very point when hope was lost, and he started writing his book *The Spiritual Man*.

After recovering a portion of his health, Nee returned to Shanghai to seek the literary assistance of his friend Ruth Lee, who had been a teacher in a Nanking college. There Lee introduced Nee to Peace Wang, the daughter of a wealthy magistrate. At the Wang home Nee, Lee, Wang and Charles Judd, an accountant with the inter-denominational China Inland Mission, met in a manner like the early church, when it was the custom of believers to meet in homes. This group in 1927 became the first

Christian "assembly place" founded on Nee's principle of locality.

From there the work quickly spread, and many local churches were founded. The rapid success of Nee's indigenous church movement was due to a number of factors: anti-Western feelings in China during the 1920s and 1930s; interdenominational rivalries, which disheartened many faithful natives; the rise of the indigenous church movement in its varied forms;* and the church's neglect of the spiritual aspect of Christianity in its deference to agrarian and educational programs. But certainly Nee's gifted preaching and teaching and the real sense of brotherhood expressed by the "Little Flock" congregations† were also responsible.

As has been described earlier, Nee had had some contact with the "London Group" of Brethren. This relation-

---

*Peter S. Goertz in his Ph.D. dissertation, "A History of the Chinese Indigenous Christian Church under the American Board in Fukien Province" (Yale University, 1933), pp. 5-6, lists the four prevailing opinions of the meaning of indigenous church:

1. Those most antiwestern in sentiment preferred a church whose founder was a native Oriental.

2. Many Westerners felt that those churches already in China are indigenous by their very nature despite its financial or organizational manner.

3. The London Missionary Society early in the nineteenth century developed the three-self concept. Its idea of self-supporting, self-governing and self-propagating became the official policy of the Chinese Communist government.

4. The American Methodist Church believed in an indigenous church in a national sense. The church was to be "ground in Chinese soul" but could have outside authority.

†Many cults and religious movements have capitalized on the apparent disparity between the biblical concept of fellowship and its practice in the modern church (viz., Jehovah's Witnesses, Mormons, Jesus People, charismatic movement).

ship was strengthened by the visit of a certain Mr. Charles Barlow in December 1930. Upon his return to England he relayed to a number of churches his absolute joy at meeting fellow Christians in China who had independently concluded that Brethren doctrine was basically correct. Correspondence between the two groups led to a visitation in October of 1932 of eight London Brethren. At first cautious in breaking bread with the Chinese congregation, they finally concluded that mutual fellowship was entirely consistent with their exclusivism.

In the spring of that year Nee received an invitation from Barlow to speak in England and America. Upon his arrival at Peterborough, England, Nee discovered that an elaborate speaking plan had been set up that limited his teaching opportunities to Brethren groups. Sensing that his hosts were too exclusive to permit him fellowship with non-Brethren, Nee told Barlow that he had to go to London for a week on "business." While the Brethren assumed his trip to be nonreligious, Nee's business was the Lord's. He went to the independent, evangelical Christian Fellowship Centre in Honor Oak Road, South London. T. Austin-Sparks, its head pastor and a favorite writer of Nee, was absent, but Nee did take the opportunity to break bread with the assistant pastor, George Patterson.

Beginning at the English docks, his American engagement was escorted by James Taylor, Sr., a Brooklyn, New York, Brethren leader. Barlow's enthusiasm for Nee and the "Little Flock" was not shared by Taylor. During the ocean voyage Nee expressed to him many of his own teachings on certain doctrines. To Taylor the eclectic pattern of his teachings was in serious error. Upon his arrival in New York Nee gave a sermon (on deliverance) which Taylor felt was deficient doctrinally. By the time Nee had reached China a more serious charge was brought by Taylor. He had discovered, quite by accident, that Nee had fellowship with non-Brethren. The Brethren quickly broke off relationships with the Chinese congregations and its leader.

Nee had also become disenchanted by their "spiritual pride," and likened them to the Laodicean Church in the Book of Revelation.[35] In his typically anthropological manner, he criticized them for "their excessive stress of the objective truth [perfection in Christ] and neglect of the subjective truth [the ongoing, inner work of the Holy Spirit]."[36]

The Brethren were too objective, whereas the Chinese Pentecostal movement suffered from an excessive subjectivity, according to Nee. Its emphasis on power, Nee felt, was regrettable. In a booklet first published in 1933 he warned others "to discern in a meeting if a person's power is psychical or spiritual."[37] Personally, he did not oppose speaking in tongues and in 1935 became involved with the movement through the mission of Miss Elizabeth Fischbacher of the China Inland Mission.

At that time she began to counsel Nee, who was seeking further spiritual power to overcome many missionary frustrations. In spite of his fundamental reservation to the instruction of men by women, he found peace and spiritual blessing in her message and some experiences associated with her Pentecostal theology.

"I have met the Lord," he wrote shortly afterwards. But

did Nee himself speak in tongues? Witness Lee, in his small booklet *The Baptism in the Holy Spirit,* writes:

> Brother Nee has never spoken in tongues. Once he sent me a cable with only the words: "Not all speak in tongues." He has studied the Word very thoroughly. I have never met a man so well versed in the scripture as he. He has found it unmistakenly clear that "not all speak in tongues." To insist all must speak in tongues is unscriptural, but to say that speaking in tongues is dispensationally over is also wrong."[38]

What Mr. Lee has said conveys quite well Watchman Nee's own feelings. In his books on biblical psychology he warned others against estatic religious experiences related to the animal elements of the human *psuchē,* which does not produce resurrection life (*zōē*).[39] Mrs. Carol Stearns, one of Nee's closest non-Oriental friends who lived in China, in an interview agreed that Nee never spoke in tongues.[40]

Nee saw in Mrs. Fischbacher and other Pentecostals a real personal faith in Jesus Christ. He never regarded speaking in tongues as unbiblical, but he did react to many of the excesses that accompany charismatic worship.[41] According to Mrs. Stearns, Nee prayed to God that He would not give him the gift of tongues, because he did not want himself to be identified with the Pentecostals in the South.*

---

*Stearns, interview. The Pentecostal movement arrived in China in 1907. In that year Nettie Moomau, a participant in the Azusa Street Revival in Los Angeles, started a revival in Hong Kong that eventually reached the southern provinces of Kwangtung, Kwangsi and Yunnan. From that time onwards the South represented a center of denominational Pentecostalism.[42]

During the time of Nee's close association with Mrs. Fischbacher, Keswick theology became a more influential part of his theological teaching. In fact, with Fischbacher's assistance, Nee attended the 1938 Keswick Convention. In its commemorative volume Nee was remembered for uttering a prayer for peace between China and Japan.[43] It was during and after his visit to England and other European countries that the addresses contained in Nee's most popular volume, *The Normal Christian Life,* were given. At the center of this book's ideas is the exegesis of Romans 7 according to the Keswick Movement.[44]

The Little Flock and the Revolution

From the beginning of his active ministry Nee shared with many of the Chinese Communist leaders a distrust of the organizational system of Protestant and Catholic missions—its wealth, its dependence upon foreign resources and its hierarchical structure. If any church or mission were so well established that its workers received salaries, that a building for worship was constructed and maintained, that charitable funds were available in reserve and that fund raising was organized and institutionalized, how could it trust in the Lord for its needs? If a worker in the church, such as Nee, had been under salary, then he would have had "his hope in men," and when their resources dried up, his resources would have dried up, too.[45] But while the Communists innately rejected any form of Christianity and placed their trust in a new political system, Nee proposed a new *ekklēsia* dependent upon the Lord for its needs.

During a conference held in 1938 in Shanghai and

Hankow he delivered a series of messages to "the inner circle of my [Nee's] most intimate associates in the work," in which he examined the biblical teaching on the church and its expression in his own ministry.[46] As for the minister's financial needs, Nee said, ". . . there are evidently two ways by which the needs of God's servants may be met—either they look to God to touch the hearts of His children to give what is needful, or they can earn it by doing part-time 'secular' work."[47] The latter method Nee considered as an option "in special circumstances."

In 1942 Nee considered the circumstances critical. Commercial trade outside of China had been nearly eliminated by the Japanese occupation of the eastern seaboard, and finances within unoccupied China were limited. Feeling that the church should not be burdened with providing him with material needs, he accepted an invitation to help in the administration of his brother George's chemical factory. The job provided income for himself and other Christians he hired, and it may have served as one means of overcoming his professional boredom as a result of twenty-two years of church work.[48]

The company expanded as wartime needs for sulfanilamide, its chief product, increased, and Nee's work there became full time. The elders at the Hardoon Road, Shanghai, assembly asked him to stop preaching until he had given up his job.* This brief association with capitalism and his subsequent "turning over" of the factory to

---

*C.T. Chan's study of his uncle gives us an anecdotal description of the factory (financial difficulties and intracompany embezzlement) and Watchman's personality (in the face of business pressure) during this five-year interim in Nee's ministry.[49]

the church would bring the "Little Flock" in disfavor with the Communist authorities after the fall of the Kuomintang.

In 1938 Nee told his fellow workers:

> It is perfectly in order for one or more members of a church to run a hospital or a school or to be responsible for mission-work, but not for any church as a whole. A church exists for the purpose of mutual help in one place, not for the purpose of bearing responsibility of work in different places. According to God's Word, all the work is the personal concern of individual brothers called and commissioned by God, as members of the Body, and not the concern of any church as a body. The responsibility of the work is always borne by one or more individuals.[50]

If institutions of social welfare were excluded from church control, it was even truer of profitable enterprises. Nee and all the assemblies also believed that those churches founded by the apostles are based upon the ground of locality. They are "intensely local," and in organization "the churches are totally independent of one another." Only in the spiritual life are they one and interdependent as the universal church.[51]*

But in 1947 Nee was no longer a leader in the local church movement or in the Shanghai assembly. The church there had been reestablished by a former bookstore worker, Witness Lee. Feeling the call of God and desiring to build upon an everlasting kingdom, Nee returned to the church that year. As for the factory that he

---

*For a more complete summary and evaluation of Nee's ecclesiology, see chapter 5.

now managed, he saw it as an opportunity to provide for the work of the church. Nee consigned all the property to the church, contrary to the teaching of 1938. By this action Nee quickly returned to a place of favor in the flock and began to preach and teach.

The preaching emphasis changed under Nee and Lee. Where once the basis of unity among the brethren was symbolized by the phrase "breaking of bread," it was now demonstrated by the "handing over" principle. The church no longer could say, "Silver and gold have I none," for now the church owned factories, turned over by its members to the control of the elders chosen from the congregation. Ecclesiastical structure changed as the work and its workers, instead of locality, became the foundation of authority. The doctrinal reversal was systematized in the "Jerusalem principle" established in February of 1948. First suggested by Lee, this plan called for the founding of a missionary center in Foochow and other large cities that would send out a host of workers to one area as a form of saturation evangelism.

Nee's popularity rose dramatically, but others dissented from the church's change of emphasis. Nee's own nephew became disillusioned by the growing idolization of Watchman.[52] Lyall even reports that the clicking that accompanied Nee's speech because of his loose-fitting dentures was often unconsciously imitated in prayer.[53]*

As the period of religious freedom was drawing to an end, the assembly places expanded dramatically. As their

---

*I observed a similar phenomena among the older Chinese Christians who attended the assembly in Hollis, New York, that was founded by Nee's associate, Stephen Kaung.

own numbers dwindled, denominational leaders expressed divided opinion on the Christian witness of the movement. Patterson and Wang[54] agreed that its members' "love for God and for each other sets a wonderful example."[55] Notson and Paton[56] were far less sympathetic and depicted them as heretical or "helplessly subject to the manipulation" of its leaders.[57] But both felt that the rise of the movement reflected the denominational churches' own shortcomings. Paton, an Anglican, wrote, "It is a tragedy that catholic order and the freedom of the Spirit were ever opposed to each other; and it would not have happened if we had not exported to China our torn and mutilated Western postmedieval Christian tradition."[58]

Nee's Imprisonment

Much has been written in the past few years in Christian literature concerning Watchman Nee's imprisonment and death. Since the purpose of this book is to examine the direction and origins of specific teachings, it is not necessary to repeat a detailed account of the historical events. Certain facts are, however, significant in an evaluation of the success and future of Nee's teachings.

On October 1, 1949, Mao Tse-tung declared the establishment of the People's Republic of China. The Koumintang government, sympathetic to Christian missions, had fled, and for those Christians who remained in their homeland it was a time of immense tension, as described by an eyewitness:

> That first summer was a strange time. Business was almost at a standstill. We were cut off from the outside world. The once crowded harbor was almost empty, and

the streets had not half of their previous traffic. Yet daily life went on with not so many outward changes. For some reason the Communists did not interfere with life in Shanghai nearly so much or so soon as in smaller towns and in the country. People coming into the city from the interior would say: "Oh, you have not been properly liberated yet. You can still do what you like, you are almost free!"

. . . A feeling of tension was kept up by the constant reports of mass arrests and executions; and almost daily one saw truckloads of wretched men and women, crouching on the floor, being hurried away to judgement.[59]

Yet in the assembly places the "work" continued. Teaching seminars became the central concern of Nee's own ministry, in order to equip the saints for the difficulties ahead.

When accusation meetings were convened under government direction in the Christian assemblies, it became evident that policies and practices within the Little Flock had made the organization vulnerable to anti-imperialistic campaigns. The September 30, 1951, issue of the Communist *Tien Feng Magazine* reported the beginning of accusation meetings against the church and particularly against its leader Watchman Nee, as an imperialist.

Nee sensed that the end was near and spent almost all his time preparing studies. Proofs on the existence of God and practical studies on the nature of Christ's righteousness, the wisdom and glory of God that is inherited by the believer and the power of Christ's resurrection were dictated to Ruth Lee and two assistants.[60] When the Communists took over Shanghai, Nee studied extensively the writings of Marx and Engels for a month, and in a series of lectures he openly told the congregation that the Marxist system was shallow compared to the perfection of Christ and was incompatible with Christian ideals.[61] But cooperation with the new government on the lines of Romans 13, he taught, was within the character of the normal Christian life.[62] His last instruction to the church was to nullify its association with business, saying: "Tell them in Hong Kong to disassociate all secular business enterprise from the church."[63] But the command came too late.

After being ordered out of Shanghai, he was arrested in Manchuria by the Department of Public Safety on April 10, 1952. He was charged with participating in five corrupt business practices. On January 18, 1956, as part of its plan to destroy the open meetings of the Little Flock, Nee was further charged with activities hostile to government policies, financial irregularities and multiple counts of adultery. The charges of capitalism were specified at that time and included bribing tax officials, stealing state secrets and having unauthorized contracts in Hong Kong and in Taiwan with the "bandit Chiang."[64] On April 12, 1952, Nee began serving a fifteen-year sentence. With its leader in prison the assembly of Shanghai excommunicated Nee, and those continuing to worship within the assembly buildings joined the Three-Self Movement. The rest of the church went underground and survived the Cultural Revolution that saw the end of outward expressions of worship.

Contrary to reports of torture and mutilation, Nee was given a sufficient diet to serve the state as a translator of

English chemical journals. In May 1968 a Red Chinese official requested political asylum. He told authorities that while serving as a prison guard in Shanghai, Watchman Nee had converted him to Jesus Christ.[65] If his statement is true, it testifies to Nee's faithfulness to his Christian hope. On June 1, 1972, four years later, Watchman Nee died and received the reward for his patience and suffering.

Some have speculated that his death was not from natural causes. His death, they postulate, occurred as the result of President Nixon's trip to China in February of 1972. During the trip someone asked a Chinese official about the condition of Watchman Nee. It is theorized that in order to avoid further embarrassment the government executed him and reported his death from a heart attack.

It is true that a number of Christian reporters accompanied the president to China, and one of the Christian newsmen, acting as their representative, did ask a Chinese representative about Nee.* But in 1972 Nee was in very ill health. He was sixty-nine years old and suffered from a heart condition. In addition to prison conditions[66]† Nee had despaired over the recent death of his wife. In a letter dated May 22, 1972, he told his sister-in-law that he was in ill health but that nevertheless his "inward joy" surpassed everything.[67] The evidence for any political

---

*As is the custom the official changed the subject and avoided any further discussion on the matter. Emmet C. McKowen, U.S. Information Agency to Dana Roberts, December 12, 1975.

†Nee spent twenty years at Shanghai First Municipal Prison. In April 1972 Nee was transferred to an open center further inland. For a description of prison conditions see n. 66.

execution seems circumstantial. Even if this were the case, the responsibility for such an action would rest totally upon the Chinese and not with the reporter.

Work of Nee's Followers

The weight and character of Nee's teachings are evident in the Little Flock in and out of China. In China the movement survives because of its religious roots independent of a hierarchical structure in which a government might attempt to impose its own will. Unlike many of the denominations in China at the time, it was grounded upon an inner life where the heart seeks a life in God.

In *Further Talks on the Church Life* Nee discovered in the Book of Acts a method of evangelism where a representative part of the church migrated to another area.* When the Flock was forced to leave the city and find refuge in the countryside or outside of China, the church saw the persecution as an opportunity to evangelize unreached areas.

Outside of China the Little Flock Movement grew openly through local evangelism and a publishing ministry. In Asia its members are found in most Chinese settlements. Parading in the streets in "gospel shirts" decorated with Bible passages colored green, they have called others to believe: "Who will accept Jesus? Who will do the Lord's work?"[69] In America and England a number of assemblies have been established—based upon Nee's principles of locality, authority by a group of elders without a pastor/

---

*"Whether a migration is peaceful or due to persecution, it is nevertheless a migration. The way of Jerusalem is to migrate; the only difference is that they went out because of persecution."[68]

rector, unstructured charismatic worship and evangelism—through the sending out of "workers" or by the distribution of books to Christians by Nee or his two fellow workers, Witness Lee and Stephen Kaung.

Stephen Kaung, a former worker in Chungking, fled China with a number of Little Flock members and established an assembly in Hollis, New York, a section of the borough of Queens.

The present assembly involves approximately 200 worshipers, who are of Chinese, Spanish and English descent. Its service includes singing, extemporaneous prayer, meditation upon Scripture in which members openly reflect upon its meaning,* a sermon delivered by one of the church elders, and the "Lord's Supper" with a common cup and a concluding "Love Feast" of food reflecting the international quality of the congregation.

Unlike Nee's original teachings, they do not consider their church as the only true church in the area. The church has no name by its doors, simply called by the believers "the assembly hall," in order that its name may not serve as a basis of division from other churches.

In keeping with its teachings on missions, the church has "sent out" Rev. Kaung to minister in the Washington, D.C., area. There Kaung assists in the building up of another congregation, leads Bible classes for a Full Gospel Business Men's Fellowship,† writes books and continues

---

*See Nee's teachings on the ministry of the Word in chapter 3.

†Established in 1953 by dairy businessman Demos Shakarian, the Full Gospel Business Men's Fellowship International is an interdenominational organization which promotes the Pentecostal experience through banquets, luncheons and conventions in a manner appealing to "blue and white collar" workers.70

the work of translating Watchman Nee's teachings into English.

Both of Kaung's present publications testify to the influence on his exegetical style of his former teacher and senior co-worker, Watchman Nee. In *The Song of Degrees,* Psalms 120-34 are taken as an occasion to describe the progressive "ascent of the soul," which leads to the believer's unity with God the Father. Beginning with Psalm 125, believers "begin to perceive that within ourselves there is that which is of the Spirit and that which is of the flesh."[71] The strategy and victory herein described is similar to that given by Nee in *The Spiritual Man* and *The Release of the Spirit.*

In *The Splendor of His Ways,* the Book of Job is interpreted in similar anthropological language. All four of Job's earthly counselors are understood as both outward and inward representations of our religious consciousness, even though he believes the narration to be a historical account.

	Outward	*Inward*
Eliphaz[72]	mysticism	emotion of the soul
Bildad[73]	traditionalism	mind of the soul
Zophar[74]	dogmatism	will of the soul
Elihu[75]	spiritual life	human spirit

Thus anthropological concerns predominate in Kaung's teachings and give further testimony to the significance of the concept of man in Nee's theology.

Witness Lee
Much of the controlling leadership of the Little Flock

Movement is now in the hands of another of Nee's colleagues, Witness Lee. From his position as an elder in a newly formed Taiwan local church congregation in 1951, his authority has grown to include twenty-six churches in the United States and numerous local churches in Germany, England, Korea, the Philippines, New Zealand and Hong Kong. His leadership and teaching have come under some sharp criticism from people within and outside of the local church phenomena.

James Mo-Oi Cheung, in his book *The Ecclesiology of Watchman Nee and Witness Lee,* accused Lee of unorthodox teachings.[76] A few months after its first printing in 1972 the book was removed from the market when it was discovered that Cheung had made some serious errors in his thesis. Watchman Nee's book *The Glorious Church* had been wrongly assigned to the authorship of Witness Lee.[77] An extensive appendix containing spurious or unsubstantiated statements about Lee had been used as a resource to interpret the state of Lee's heterodoxy.[78] Cheung's contrast between Nee and Lee was therefore somewhat invalidated by the research inexactness.

In a series of four articles in *Nan Pei Chi,* a Hong Kong news magazine, comparable in style and popularity to that of *Newsweek,* two anonymous writers gave an extensive account of certain irregularities in the work of a Little Flock leader identified by subterfuge as Wit X Lee.[79] In the serial Lee is accused of:

1. Political and economic activities, which were the basis of Nee's imprisonment.
2. Using Nee's greatness to foster his own religious kingdom in Asia and in the United States.

3. Taking Christians to civil court (contrary to 1 Cor. 6:1-11) in order to gain control of a congregation and its church property.

While it is perhaps difficult to prove the first allegation, and the second is merely an interpretation of motives, the events of the conspiracy described in the article are well-known facts in Hong Kong as the result of newspaper publicity. Such activities are certainly in sharp contrast to Nee's own submissive nature,* and it is indeed a pity that many in Asia and America see him as the spiritual and intellectual successor to Watchman Nee.

Among the American churches Lee's authority is not evident in any form of monarchial system of ecclesiology in which he serves as the chief apostle or archbishop. It is much more subtle than that. Each church has a number of teaching elders (as they see it), according to God's dispensation of charisms. The congregation outwardly recognizes this by their harmonious shouts of "Amen!" and "Hallelujah!" during the delivery of his Bible exposition or sermon. Despite their strong assertions to the contrary, much of the content and form of these "inspired teachings" comes from reading Nee's and Lee's books. Since Lee is still living, most, if not all, of the elders attend one of his "training" sessions. Here they receive intensified instruction on interpreting a portion of Scripture by one's

---

*In *The Normal Christian Church Life*, Nee writes: "When an apostle comes to a place where a local church already exists, he must never forget that no church authority rests with him. Should he desire to work in a place where the local church does not wish to have him, then all he can do is to pass on to some other part" (p. 80). Nee readily accepted such church decisions in his own ministry.

"spirit-reading"* of the Bible. Since Lee is the best interpreter of Nee's teachings and the Bible, diversity is difficult. In one meeting I asked an elder if he reads anything on the Bible other than the writings of Nee and Lee. He replied, "Yes, you mean Jessie Penn-Lewis, some of us read her books."

"But what about Christian writers like Wesley, F.F. Bruce, Schaeffer or even Thomas à Kempis?" I asked.

"We cannot be sure about these people," he replied. "Why should we read them if we already have the truth?"

By his remarks this elder demonstrates the all-encompassing influence of Nee and Lee's instruction on anthropology.[80] Since both men have shown the proper way of determining what insights are of the human spirit enlightened by the Holy Spirit and what are of the soul, other books are "mixed" products—among their inspired insights there are soulish, unspiritual elements.

But Lee's messages lack much of the polish and intellectual care so typical of Nee's writings. On Gal. 1:4, Lee writes:

> Many Bible translators translate the Greek word for age into world, because an age is a part or period of the whole world. All the ages added together equal the world. During the time of the Apostle Paul, there was a certain age. If you have ever read the world history of that period of time, you could see that the age had three aspects: Greek philosophy, Roman politics, and the Hebrew religion. The Greeks brought in the philosophy, the wisdom and the knowledge. The Romans brought in the way to govern and organize a strong administration. Then the

---

*See chapter 3 for Nee's teachings on the ministry of the Word.

Hebrews had the best religion.

Now we can see that what Paul means when he speaks of the present evil age is the Hebrew religion.[81]

But if someone were to interject that such an interpretation is inconsistent with the biblical usage of *aiōn*,[82] those adhering to Lee's theology would reply that such an objection is according to religion and not according to Christ:

> Religion, politics, the faith, and scriptural interpretation must all pass away for us. Christ has the answer to each of these questions, but he does not care for; neither must we care for anything but the living Lord, the living Christ. As long as we have His presence, it is sufficient. We must learn just to turn to our spirit and say, O Lord! This is the way to experience Him.[83]
>
> . . . When I was young I did much searching and researching of the Bible. But, Hallelujah, today I have given it up. . . .[84]

The mark of this Christocentrism in today's "Small Flock" or "local church" congregations is rather vague in Lee's books, but it appears to be interrelated with his dogmatic assertions about the need for all believers to see the doctrine of locality, to say "Amen" and "Hallelujah" in the congregational worship and to be able to discern between soul and spirit. Like Nee and Kaung, biblical anthropology according to a trichotomous division plays an important part in his theology. Avoidance of objective methods of biblical study and an outright denial of evangelical hermeneutics[85] has caused Lee to accept unorthodox ritual within his local churches. He writes:

> In the beginning of 1968 something really happened in

Los Angeles. The burial. It was the time of the New Year Conference, and I had no intention of encouraging people to be buried. But at the closing of one meeting, one said, "I want to be buried," then others followed until many brothers and sisters in the church were buried. They were all so deeply moved to testify by this act that they were burying all their oldness, and by doing this they became alive. I was really surprised by this move to be buried. I was trying, in fact, to say some word to stop it, but I was checked by the Spirit within. Who was I to stop something of the Holy Spirit? I said not a word until the third day, when I predicted that the church in Los Angeles would certainly be criticized by the religious people for this act. It was not more than ten days before the criticism came. "There is heresy in Los Angeles," they said. "Believers who are already properly baptized are being baptized again. Where is the scriptural ground for a believer to be baptized again after being properly baptized already?" I do not like to argue, but I wish to tell you that so many withered "hands" were healed. Not only did this occur in Los Angeles, but followed this in many places, many dead ones through this kind of burial came alive. What can we say?[86]

Are Lee's assemblies heretical? Clearly it has many of the characteristics of "heresy" described both by Schlier and Farrer[87]—lack of love toward fellow believers, self-assertiveness, a self-chosen authority of a teacher and an authoritative stand on a disputable doctrine(s) (e.g., repeated baptisms, ecclesiology, tripartite anthropology, and biblical interpretation). As will be seen in the following chapters, Lee's experiential hermeneutics, doctrinal

laissez faire and absolute exclusiveness are contrary to
the theological balance presented in the content of the
entire literary production of Watchman Nee.

2

Introduction to Nee's Literature

Watchman Nee's faithfulness to his beliefs in the face of political hostility and his position as a Chinese church leader contributed greatly to his significance in the history of the church. Nevertheless, it is the publication of his Bible studies that have been most responsible for the popularity that has occurred subsequent to his public ministry. Presently (September 1978) forty-three volumes have appeared in English, with an indeterminate amount in preparation.

Of these books only his three-volume study, *The Spiritual Man,* was originally written in book form. The rest of the titles are the result of editing of two other sources: Nee's magazine articles and the notes of his lectures.

Nee edited four different Christian magazines: *The Revival* (1922-25, 1931-48), *The Christian* (1925-30), *The Bible Record* (ca. 1925) and *The Ministry* (June 1948-?). The format of these periodicals was by and large modeled after Jessie Penn-Lewis's *The Overcomer* and T. Austin-Sparks's *A Witness and A Testimony:* (1) an editorial[1]* by Nee or another co-worker, (2) a long excerpt from the writings of Andrew Murray, F.B. Meyer

---

*See Appendix B.

or one of the other devotional writers he had become familiar with, and (3) a Bible study prepared from Nee's spoken ministry or, in some instances, articles written specifically for the magazine.

A preponderance of his material comes from English and Mandarin shorthand* notes taken during his many lectures in China and abroad. Some were edited by Nee and printed in his magazines and booklets, thereby receiving the benefit of his own authorization. Other texts have only recently been published into Chinese and a host of other languages. While these notes provide us with a prolific source of Nee's theology, the messages are more vulnerable to alterations as the result of editing.

For example, in *Twelve Baskets Full,* volume three, chapters ten and eleven are designated by the anonymous editor as "Selections from *The Normal Christian Life.*" But if we compare this text with that of Kinnear's full text edition, it is evident that the edited text has been trimmed down by taking sentences from different paragraphs and joining them into new cohesive paragraphs. Carefully done, this form of editing can be an appropriate form of abridgment. In one instance the editor does leave in a complete anecdote by Nee, which provides us with two comparable variations. (See next page.)

How are these differences to be explained? The reference to "preaching in the villages of China" could well have been omitted for purposes of editing. But what

---

*A less complicated system than the ancient "regular" form of writing, Mandarin shorthand (Kuan Hua Tzu Mu) contains only 70 characters instead of the usual 4,000.[2] Miss Elizabeth Fischbacher recorded Nee's messages in direct translation into English.[3]

I remember once I took up a small book and put a piece of paper into it, and I said to those very simple folk [Chinese villagers], "Now look carefully. I take a piece of paper. It has an identity of its own, quite separate from this book. Having no special purpose for it at the moment I put it into the book. Now I do something with the book. I post it to Shanghai. I do not post the paper, but the paper has been put into the book. Then where is the paper? Can the book go to Shanghai and the paper remain here? Can the paper have a separate destiny from the book? No! Where the book goes the paper goes. If I drop the book in the river the paper goes too, and if I quickly take it out again I recover the paper also. Whatever the experience the book goes through the paper goes through with it, for it is still there in the book."

"Of him are ye in Christ Jesus."[4]

For instance, I put a treasury note in my Bible. Now I mail the Bible to Shanghai. Can the Bible get to Shanghai and the note remain here? No; where the Bible goes the note goes, and whatever the Bible goes through, the note goes through too, for it is in the Bible. "Of him are ye in Christ Jesus."[5]

caused the "book"/"Bible"* and "paper"/"treasury note" textual variations? These variants are not the result of differences in translation. It seems unlikely that the texts are from two different lectures, since Nee believed that a minister should never repeat his sermons.[6]

Annotated Bibliography

Before systematically examining his epistemology, anthropology and ecclesiology, it is important first to understand the historical order and direction of the literature from his teaching ministry. All of these works can be chronologically divided into three periods of theological development: the period from 1927 to 1935, from 1936 to 1945 and from 1946 to 1951.

Spiritual Growth

In the early period, from 1927 to 1935, according to Nee's own testimony, the work was "to assist God's children in their spiritual life and spiritual warfare."[7] There is little instruction on the operation of the church but rather instruction in the means of personal spiritual growth through a reassessment of the biblical evidence of God's working in human nature. The theology of this period is not original, for it is easily identifiable with Plymouth Brethren and Keswick exegesis.

In *The Spiritual Man* Nee presents his most thorough interpretation of biblical anthropology. By further distinguishing the functions of the human spirit into intuition, communion and conscience, and of the soul into emotion,

---

*In Mandarin the Bible is Sheng[4]-Shu[1] and book is Shu[1].

mind and will, Nee feels the believer can properly test whether religious practices are of God or "soulish" deceptions. This distinguishing between "soulical" and "spiritual" conduct permeates all of his messages on Christian maturity and influences all his theology.

During 1930/31, Nee prepared a series of fifty questions and answers on Bible doctrines, posthumously published as *Gospel Dialogue*. Grace, sin, justification, sanctification, forgiveness, the atonement and perfection are defined in a manner similar to Keswick's admixture of Calvinism and perfectionism.

At about the same time the messages in *Spiritual Reality or Obsession* were given. Containing only sixty-four pages in its present publication format, the work is a prolegomenon to his ideas on the nature of our spiritual knowledge within the church. For the Christian there are only two choices in relation to spiritual truth. He will either be "obsessed"/deceived into upholding falsehood instead of truth, or he will touch the "reality" of God through the guidance of the Holy Spirit working in the inner man. This working of God in the individual is undertaken by walking in the light of God and is a salient feature of Keswick and Brethren writers who have been influenced by evangelical pietism.[8]

In the summer of 1932, before Nee had any personal contact with Pentecostals, he wrote a series of articles in *Revival Magazine* questioning the origins of tongues, parapsychic phenomena and the ecstatic practices of other religions. Relying on the conclusions of Mrs. Penn-Lewis's *Soul and Spirit* and G.H. Pember's *Earth's Earliest Ages,* the articles are a sequel to the tripartite theology of *The Spiritual Man* and have been republished collectively in *The Latent Power of the Soul.*

In 1934 Nee gave a Bible study in Hankow, China, in which the Song of Songs was interpreted in terms of spiritual communion. His interpretations (*The Song of Songs*) are a continuation of his concern for the reality of the spiritual life in the church. The material seems to be an integration of Penn-Lewis's commentary, *Thy Hidden Ones* and Mr. C.A. Coates's *An Outline of the Song of Solomon.* Nee is careful to study the actual content of the text and avoids both the overspiritualization of Mrs. Penn-Lewis and the false "shepherd hypothesis."*

Nee again underlined the need for spiritual reality in a series of messages (*Spiritual Knowledge*) focusing on the way to true self-understanding. This self-understanding is not undertaken by psychoanalytic introspection but by God revealing the need for our minds to be renewed and our hearts to be circumcised. The method for this transformation of the Christian personality is God's working in the inner man as understood in Nee's trichotomous anthropology.

The Antioch Principle

By the summer of 1937 the Japanese had begun their World War II drive into the heartland of China. With a large migration of refugees and the opportunity open to evangelize in other parts of the country, Nee realized the necessity of establishing some form of guidelines for the structure and missionary work of his local church. The

---

*In this interpretation there are three principle characters in The Song of Solomon: Solomon, the Shulamite maiden and her shepherd lover.[9]

church must now be instructed in the truths contained in the Corinthian Epistles (polity), as Nee saw it, in addition to the Word from the Ephesian Epistle (sanctification). Consecration and church vocational guidance are also an important part of this teaching period. Within the next three and a half years, ten volumes were produced, representing his most popular and probably his most original material.

Before this, any one of the churches established by Watchman Nee could accurately be described as a lay sect established on Brethren principles of opposition to professional clergy, to extralocal authority, to denominationalism and to formal membership, with an additional emphasis on the spiritual life of the individual. A change came as a result of the teachings offered in *The Normal Christian Church Life* (original title: *Rethinking Our Missions*). After examining the activities of his own work and the evidence of Scripture, Nee suggested guidelines of church order for his mission-oriented churches. Apostles were missionaries who by the charism administered by God and by the recognition of the church served in the sphere of the church universal. The elders were the leaders of the church local. Since the church at Antioch in the Book of Acts was the most missionary-conscious of the New Testament churches, it should be the model of the Chinese Church. Furthermore, since no city or town is described as having two congregations, there must be one church for one locality.

His unique emphasis on the "ground of locality" created no controversy among the members of the Little

Flock churches.* As a minority movement in a minority
religion Nee's churches were still too small and economi-
cally too weak to have more than one church in one
location. The movement's singleness of purpose (building
up God's church in love) prevented the congregations
from developing any schismatic diversity. Even after
Nee's local church movement had become a divided sect,
"locality" became the doctrine and pattern of the mission
work. Any church formed apart from these principles
was considered to be in error. Even in the book *The
Normal Christian Church Life,* which Mo-Oi Cheung
regarded as the written expression of Nee's church local,
what matters most is not ecclesiastical methods but the
nature of man:

> . . . what matters most is the man, not his methods.
> Unless the man is right right methods will be of no use to
> him or his work. Carnal methods are suited to carnal men,
> and spiritual methods to spiritual men. For carnal men to
> employ spiritual methods will only result in confusion
> and failure.[10]

Two books came out of his trip to Europe the following
year. *The Normal Christian Life* describes the progress of
the believer towards the goal of absolute surrender to
God according to Romans 5-8. The publishers introduce
the work as "a spiritual classic,"[11] and indeed the
American edition has already sold well over 600,000
copies. The central theme is one of a progressive
Godward "abiding in Him," yet as is characteristic of
Nee's exegesis, chapter seven dwells at length upon

---

*From here on Nee's assemblies shall be called the local churches.

God's response to the spirit and the soul.

Sit, Walk, Stand has much of this same emphasis on spiritual growth. Here Nee summarizes the message of Ephesians, according to Paul's distinctive use of verbs,* relative to the soteriological disposition of the believer. Speaking to Holiness groups in England and Europe, these messages were heard by receptive ears. His theology is totally that of the Keswick teaching, with a gracious and illustrative style equal to that of Andrew Murray and F.B. Meyer.

A series of addresses on the Christian's attitude toward the world given from 1938 to 1941, together with a few adjunctive sermons, comprise the book *Love Not the World.* Enroth, Ericson and Peters, in their study of the Jesus People, have unduly criticized this book for its "anti-cultural fundamentalism."[12] Nee makes no apologies for his disappointment that the earth's resources have fallen into "unconsecrated hands."[13] The solution is not the world-abandoning escapism of such premillennial cults as the Children of God, but:

> . . . today the church has a definite responsibility before God to register the victory of Christ in the Devil's territory. If there is to be a testimony to the principalities and powers, if the impact of Christ's sovereignty through His Cross is to be registered in the spiritual realm, it can only be as the judicial foothold in our hearts of the "pretender" in the race is met, and by the same Cross, removed and repudiated. For God's object is still that man should "have dominion." Our work for Him does not stop

---

*The three verbs are in 1:20, 2:6 (*Kathizō/sugkathizō*); 4:1, 17; 5:2, 8 (*peripateō*); and 6:11, 13, 14 (*histemi*).

with proclaiming a Gospel that was designed merely to undo the effect of Genesis 3, marvellous as was that undoing. God wants also to take us back further to Genesis 1 itself.[14]

Nee continues by saying that the purification of the world is coincident with the consecration of the spirit: "Godward that in itself effectually deprives Satan of any moral ground in us he may claim to possess."[15]

Another important theme arising out of Nee's messages is recognizing God's call for service—illustratively expressed in *What Shall This Man Do?*. There are only three emphases of ministry in the New Testament. Whether God calls a worker to minister in the style of Peter (the proclaimer of salvation who serves as the fisher of men), Paul (the tentmaker, the builder of God's house) or John (as a mender of nets, he restores the churches) depends upon the will of God preparing him even before the believer's renaissance. For Paul says, "Let each man abide in that calling wherein he was called."[16] And for Nee this abiding comes about as we are open to the Lord's many opportunities to enlarge our ministry. It is more a question of letting God activate us in His body than our determining our ministry's course and function.

Beginning at the end of the year 1939 Nee gave five lectures on Christ and His relationship to the believer. As its English title suggests (*Christ The Sum of All Spiritual Things*) a high Christology is proposed:

One day I was talking to a group of people about this spiritual fact. As I spoke, many eyes stared at me. I told them I would present a most significant fact to them; namely, that God's Christ is God's everything, for God has nothing else but Christ! God has not given us light, He gives Christ to us; God has not given us food, He gives Christ to us; God has not given us the way, the truth, and the life, instead He gives us Christ. God's Christ is all things; aside from Him God has nothing.[17]

Such ontological abstractions here may be one source for Witness Lee's modalism.[18] Here at least Nee is orthodox enough to understand that Christ is all things in that He is the subject and sum of all our needs. God has not given us many things outside of Christ. Therefore prayers offered for healing, patience and other works of grace must be directed to the fulfillment of Christ's resurrection life in our whole being.

The homiletical style of Nee's teachings is quite evident in *Changed into His Likeness*.[19] Why is it that God tells Moses at Sinai that He is "the God of Abraham, the God of Isaac, and the God of Jacob" (Exod. 3:6)? The question actuates Nee's talents into formulating a sermon in the common three-point form. Guided by Romans 9-11 and Galatians 3ff., Nee thought this triple refrain must together represent the spiritual experience of all God's people.

Abraham was chosen by God in His sovereign grace apart from any righteousness—for Abraham was a worshiper of idols when God called him—and apart from any physical effort. For us Abraham represents our hope of reaching the final promised land.

Isaac typifies Christ in that he embodies God's plan and willingly accepts his place in God's sacrificial system, "passively." Isaac provides the transition between Abraham's life of promise and Jacob's life, which signals the transformation of human nature through Christ.

These analogies are a bit farfetched. Particularly when he sees two works of grace in the believer through Jacob's experiences at Peniel and El-bethel. Throughout this homily the contrast between the spiritual man and the natural man embodies the essential hindrance in our striving to be formed into God's likeness.

Perhaps correctly understanding wartime needs, in *God's Work*[20] Nee prepared other Christians to better comprehend the mystery of their responsibility in God's redemptive plan. For the church to survive the coming occupation it had to do more than save souls. Outwardly the church has a clear mission and command to preach the gospel, but inwardly it needs the revelation of God's will to further build up the body of Christ in order to overcome the sicknesses of this world. For without God revealing His will in the hearts of the one ministering and the one ministered to, the church's work will be ineffectual and vacant of spiritual life. Therefore, Nee believed, the church must "deeply know the cross, . . . know the cross within and bear it daily."[21] In a sense, once the body surrenders itself to the redemption of the cross, it will receive resurrection power—ever-revealing God's will for His people. "We refuse all service," Nee says, "which is only to man."[22] For as priests our service is also Godward and needs to first go through the death of the cross, which will purify us and crucify "the natural life." Once undertaken "the Lord gives us grace to enter into the Holy of Holies because all of self and all of man and all of mixture and all of earth has been destroyed in death but what is indestructible and what is deathless has emerged in resurrection life."[23] Here again Nee supports his argument with an anthropological theme: redemption through the cross working in human nature.

Shortly before the fall of Shanghai, he preached a series of five messages on prayer. Quite consistently, he begins his thesis with a talk on man's divinely pronounced authority of free will. For this reason man has a unique place and purpose in Nee's theology. Man is the only aspect of creation which can restrict the divine purpose. In God's design, Nee believes, man has been given a conscious choice between being one with, or divided from, His eternal will. In the Christian life the former is implemented through the medium of prayer—honoring God's name, inaugurating God's kingdom upon the earth and thus invoking God's will. This study was later published in the United States under the title *The Prayer Ministry of the Church.*[24]

The Jerusalem Principle

We may mark the third and final literary period with the war's end in 1945 and Nee's final resignation from the pharmaceutical firm. Shortly thereafter Nee gave an exposition on the seven churches in the Book of Revelation. His thoughts on Ephesus, Smyrna, Pergamum, Thyatira and Sardis are not very original, reflecting the historical dispensational approach, where each church is representative of God's judgment upon periods of church history.[25] With the exception of Smyrna these church ages had lost sight of the apostolic vision of the church of Jesus Christ. It is not until the advent of the Philadelphia church that the people of God "recover" the apostolic tradition.

Specifically, this new, wholly reformed church began in 1825 with the Plymouth Brethren. In the published text of this Bible study the presumed return to ecclesiastical orthodoxy included denominational and clerical iconoclasm:

> These believers, in the world's eye, were lowly and unknown. But they had the Lord in their midst and the consolation of the Holy Spirit. They stood on the ground of two clear truths: firstly, that the church is the Body of Jesus Christ and that this Body is only one; secondly, in the New Testament there is no clergy system; all the ministers of the Word set up by men are not scriptural. They believed that all true believers are the members of this one Body.[26]

These two principles are extolled in many of his books and were the guiding principles of the Little Flock. Yet Nee warned both the local churches and the Brethren of the ever-present danger of becoming lukewarm in their faithful and true witness, as did the church of Laodicea. The only preventive against this was for each member of every congregation to be an "overcomer." As chapter four will explain, he defines this overcoming state by means of an anthropological soul/spirit dialectic.

Two years later Nee gave a talk to fellow workers in Foochow on the sanctifying work of the cross through the breaking of the outward man (the soul/body) to allow the release of the spirit. The published version, *The Release of the Spirit,* has become exceedingly popular for its description of the somatic/psychic/pneumatic dynamics of the spiritual life.

In February of 1948 the "Jerusalem principle" geographically focused Nee's teaching ministry almost entirely within the city of Foochow. A total of nine books have been published from the work there.

While *The Normal Christian Church Life* presents the theoretical and political framework of Nee's concept of the church, his Basic Lesson Series[27] contains the outline and guidelines of the practical church life. His teachings on deliverance (Romans 7), prayer, praise, thanksgiving, the simple life, the sacraments, sex and marriage, evangelism and the conduct of worship are further explained through exposition of pertinent passages. Much of the material presented in earlier writings is summarized, and it can be said with some justification that the six volumes of the series represent a collation of his practical theology. As such, Nee avoids the anthropological emphasis of his earlier works. He provides in the fourth volume:

> During the past twenty years, I have received enough letters and met enough people to certify how often Christians try to examine their inner feelings. After they are told of the separation of spirit and soul, they start to analyze themselves day in and day out. They inwardly become a laboratory where they unceasingly analyze what is right and what is not right. This is most unhealthy and is a symptom of sickness. We should not allow God's children to do that.[28]

Such cautions had been a concern with Nee since the beginning of his ministry.[29] Yet he continued to write on the subject for those capable of deriving help from such teaching. For example, *Ye Search the Scriptures,* which chronologically follows the Basic Lesson Series, is a book that deals just as much with Christian anthropology as it does with Bible study. Over half of the text discusses the preparation of the man best able to use his proposed Bible study methods. Again in *The Ministry of God's Word* the intent of the book is not so much to teach homiletic techniques but to reveal to the preacher and teacher that his flesh "must be transformed according to the requirements of God's word."[30]

Quite important to the local churches under the new "Jerusalem principle" of church organization is the question of authority.[31] In *Spiritual Authority* Nee declares that all authority comes from God. Those who rebel against authority are full of human thought and reason, and God's rule in their life is blocked. While we must submit to all authority, we are not commanded to obey those authorities who clearly command contrary to the will of God (Scripture). Instruction is given in spiritual discernment between God-delegated authority and ungodly rule.

The last book coming out of the Foochow teaching center is *The Normal Christian Worker*. Like many of his other writings, a practical set of guidelines is not his purpose but the spiritual advance of the worker's inner life. The necessary implements of service, diligence, stability, love, honesty and long-suffering are there for the worker who wishes to be free from the soulish activity and whose heart, mind and spirit are open to God's purposes.[32]

Further Talks on the Church Life is a collection of essays given in the later years of Nee's public ministry. Chapter six is the oldest essay and was given in August 1948. It contains a representation of the Jerusalem principle. The rest of the chapters are but amplifications of his ecclesiology of locality. Written after the fall of China, when church leadership seemed threatened, the themes of unity and preserving local church polity dominate the content of these, his public, messages.

Practical Issues of This Life, The Glory of His Life and *The Body of Christ: A Reality* are three collections of essays given at various times and then edited according to certain general themes. Theologically they offer little in the way of insights into the governing principles of Nee's teachings. As the first title suggests, they are examples of Nee's practical applications of the instruction given in such works as *The Normal Christian Life, The Spiritual Man* and *The Normal Christian Church Life.*

Two anthologies have been published. *A Table in the Wilderness* contains daily meditations from his writings. *Twelve Baskets Full* is a four-volume series containing "fragments" from his entire Christian life.*

The work of translation and publication continues, and it is reasonable to assume that the present list of works will be expanded to include a sizable number of future publications. While there is still much of Nee's career unaccounted for by the present publications, there is

---

*Two new books have been published too late to be included in the appropriate chronological order. *Come, Lord Jesus* is a study of The Book of Revelation. In his preface Stephen Kaung, the translator and editor, explains that his original mimeograph notes on Rev. 2:19-3:22 were missing. To provide a continuous running commentary, portions of *The Orthodoxy of the Church* were substituted. *God's Plan and the Overcomers,* written in 1934, explains how a portion of God's people will ultimately play an important part in the millennium and Christ's second coming. These two works provide much of the material used in interpreting his eschatology. See Chapter 5, "The Church in the Eschaton."

sufficient evidence from Kinnear's biography and Witness Lee's account to be confident that the fundamentals of Nee's theology are already present in the books just described.

Style

Any reader of Watchman Nee's writings is conscious of a pervasive devotional style in all but one of his works.* From the beginning Nee emphasized that his work, as is all of the church's work, is to be dominated by the "spiritual." By this Nee meant that the church must be concerned with allowing the human spirit to touch the spiritual reality, which is the church's revelation from God. All must be spiritual. "Whatever may be entered into without the guidance of the Holy Spirit," Nee says, "is definitely not spiritual reality."[33] The church achieves this reality by developing and nurturing, not the carnal man, but the spiritual man. This is the sum and substance of the literature of Watchman Nee.

---

*Only in *Come, Lord Jesus* (New York: Christian Fellowship Publishers, 1976) does the text resemble an interpretive exegesis of a biblical text.

3

The Word and Its Ministry

At the forefront of all Christian theology there is one central issue: How do we know God through His Word? Watchman Nee and his movement challenged and broke with much of what in the mission community he considered to be the traditions of men. As Karl Barth reacted to the weaknesses in German liberalism, so also Nee objected to the denominational strife and theological divisions among the different missionary societies. Nee and Barth's responses were in part a reaffirmation of the church's epistemological roots in the Word of God. But while Barth unhesitantly drew a wedge between the inerrant Word of God and the human witness of that Word in Scripture and preaching,[1] Nee sees the scriptural witnesses as inerrant through the sanctifying activity of the Holy Spirit in the spiritual man.

The Word

Nee does not specify the Word of God in a threefold form as Barth does,[2] but rather describes the Word in terms of the various ministrations found in three kinds of people. In the Old Testament the Word came to the prophets in a way that did not "mingle" with their own opinions, feelings or thoughts. God only used their voices and controlled them to the extent that the Word might not be tainted by human error. But there were Moses, Isaiah, David and Jeremiah, whose personal feelings mirrored those of God enough that they could use them to speak the Word of God. While they acted mostly under an Old Testament prophetic form, their ministry foreshadowed New Testament apostolic principles.[3]

In Jesus, the Word becomes flesh. Not only His voice but His thoughts, feelings and opinion communicated the Word. No longer is the Word objectively presented to the house of Israel alone, but it is also presented subjectively to all men. It is God's desire that His Word should carry human feelings, thoughts and ideas, through the personality of Jesus. Nee implies that the Old Testament office of prophet finds its completion in Jesus. For, "when He opened His mouth there was God's Word; even when He shut His mouth, God's Word was still there, for as a Person He is the Word of God."[4]

In Jesus, the Word is fully consistent with the flesh. In the New Testament ministry of the apostles, therefore, the flesh must be transformed according to God's Word in order that the flesh might become the instrument to communicate that Word in a divine and human form. This is the basis of the Word in the writers of the New Testament and of every Christian minister of the Word.

Nee therefore does not believe, as Barth does,[5] that the preaching of God's Word (the ministry) need be contaminated by the human element. Rather it is God's intention that the Word should be subjective by its mingling with the person who is open and obedient to God. While Barth and the neo-orthodox theologians view God's sovereignty as working in human history alone, Nee sees God working sovereignly in the inner man preparing the way of revelation, also.

In every book by Watchman Nee there is no question that he holds to the central evangelical premise: The Bible is the inspired Word of God. Unlike Barth's teachings, the Bible is not in a state of becoming,[6] for it is already the Word of God. "It reveals to us," Nee says, "all that God has done for us in the past."[7] Now it is the church's guide to lead us to God and our life in Christ.

The Word Studied

Since it is extremely rare, according to Nee, for God to speak with words not found in the Bible, Nee was concerned to "equip the saints" with the means of effectually studying the Scripture. Instruction in this area does not begin with methods and exegesis, Nee argues; the man himself must be primary:

> Consequently, in approaching this matter of searching the Scriptures, we should naturally divide it into two parts: first, the preparation of man; second, the methods of Bible study.[8]

Quoting the words of Jesus in John 6:63, Nee begins his study of the human preparation by stating that the words of the Bible are more than words, "they are also spirit."[9] It is not the unregenerate, "natural man" who can understand the meaning of the Bible. It is not for the carnal believer who has the Spirit without submitting to God's authority (his understanding of the Bible is quite limited). But it is the spiritual man who is taught in God's wisdom by the Holy Spirit, "combining spiritual things with spiritual words."[10]* He knows that the Bible is without error or contradiction. He has the Spirit's interpretation and is personally cognitive of the inner Word of God, outwardly expressed in the words of the Bible.†

This is a cardinal point in understanding the style and character of the writings of Watchman Nee and helps to explain some of the eccentric tendencies among members of the small flock churches. By their hermeneutics-of-the-spiritual-man principle, Nee and his followers are quick to reject all forms of liberalism and higher criticism. Nee writes:

> If a person is not regenerated, then no matter how clever and scholarly he may be, to him this book is a mystery. But a regenerated man whose cultural background may be quite primitive possesses greater understanding of the Bible than does an unregenerate college professor. And the explanation? One of them has a regenerate spirit, while the other has not. The Scriptures cannot be mastered through cleverness, research, or natural talent. The word of God is spirit, therefore it can only be known to whoever possesses a regenerated spirit. Since the *root* and *nature* of the Bible are spiritual, how can anyone who lacks a regenerated spirit begin to understand it? It is a closed book to him.[12]

Conservative Christianity also comes under such criticism.

---

*Nee also comments on the American Standard Version, marginal translation, "interpreting spiritual things to spiritual men." Nee's thoughts here are derived in large part from his interpretation of 1 Cor. 2-3.

†"The distinctiveness of this Book is its dual feature: on the one hand the Bible has its outer shell—the physical part of the Bible—similar to the part of man which is made of dust; on the other hand it has its spiritual part, that which is in the Holy Spirit, what is God breathed and God spoken."[11]

Much of the theological divisions among Christian churches and missions Nee attributes to individual and therefore private interpretation contrary to 2 Pet. 1:20.[13]

It is not enough to have a regenerate spirit. "Man needs not only to possess this spirit," Nee says, "but needs also to be possessed by this spirit."[14] The Spirit must also exercise his spirit, his "god-consciousness," and he must consecrate himself absolutely and entirely to the Lord. While there may be much truth in what Nee says here, the sense of his words was altered in many of the local churches as a result of the leadership vacuum created by Watchman Nee's imprisonment. Even those writers whom Nee regarded as spiritual* and those who would probably fit his criteria are now regarded by many of the local churches' members as not spiritual enough. They reason that it is a better use of one's time to read only the Bible and Bible interpreters equal to Nee's books in spiritual content. Who is equal to Nee? Among the local church groups that follow this teaching there are only two modern writers capable of writing on this spiritual plane: Watchman Nee himself and Witness Lee.

In *Ye Search the Scriptures* a number of methods of Bible study are discussed in detail. These methods and his spiritual criticism of the Bible are not very original, but are quite similar to the Keswick devotional emphasis on Bible study. One need only compare the contents of A.T. Pierson's *The Bible and Spiritual Criticism* with Nee's

---

*Among those Bible expositors Nee recommends are Henry Alford, Thomas Chalmers, J.N. Darby, Charles Finney, Jessie Penn-Lewis, Dwight L. Moody, C.H. Mackintosh, Phillip Schaff, William Smith, Hudson Taylor, R.A. Torrey, S.P. Tregelles, B.F. Westcott and Christopher Wordsworth.

book. Like Nee he also believed in the "necessity of the 'Spiritual Man' to perceive, discern and apprehend the spiritual element in the book [the Bible]."[15]

With these proper methods, in conjunction with the regenerated human spirit, the minister enters or "penetrates" into the things of the Holy Spirit in three ways.[16] First, he enters into the thought or explanation within the Bible and perceives its real meaning. Secondly, he enters into the factual impression of the Holy Spirit presented in each historical incident of the Bible as it relates to the whole working of God. Finally, he enters into the spirit of the Bible. In the Bible the Holy Spirit has manifested His own feelings through the writers' human spirits. He that is spiritual enters in and "touches" that same Spirit and experiences these same feelings. But without the initial preparation of man all study of the Bible is without life and is a dead work.

The Minister Sanctified

For Nee the Bible teaches that some men are called to be teaching-elders in the local congregation.[17] They alone are not what Nee means by the ministers of the Word; they only train people to be more effective ministers. All believers have the potential to minister in presenting the Word of God to other people. "A minister of the Word is one who has the revelation of Christ, one in whom God has been pleased to reveal His Son (see Gal. 1:16)."[18] That is, man must first by faith be brought by God to Christ for the knowledge of the Son. Without this "basic revelation" man cannot begin to know the Bible as the Word of God, nor can he impart the Word to others. This knowledge through revelation of the Son Nee describes as a "touch." Like the woman with the issue of blood in Mark 5, it is not enough for man to press around Jesus, he must touch Him "with conscious faith":

> The words which the Lord utters are spirit and life. If you touch this you touch the ministry of the word. The task is not simply presenting a book to men, rather it is presenting the Son of God in the Book. When a minister of the word serves people with God's word, he simultaneously serves with the Son of God. We minister with Christ.[19]

Many in the Church, Nee complains, have crowded around the Bible but have not touched its reality and the Christ within.

The basic revelation is essential to the apostolic post-ascension[20]* ministry, for the Word of God is both the incarnate Son of God and the printed Scriptures. The church's present ministry of the Word therefore is founded on its knowledge of Christ and its familiarity with the Bible. For this reason Nee further delimits the minister of the Word to the "one who translates Christ into the Bible; that is, he tells people of the Christ he knows in the words of the Bible so that in those who receive the Bible the Holy Spirit will translate it back into Christ."[21]

How can one receive the basic revelation? Certainly Nee means here nothing less than conversion/regeneration itself.[22] The unrepentant is unable to hear the

---

*"The Christian era began with Christ, of whom we are told that, when He had made purification of sins, He 'sat down on the right hand of the Majesty on high' (Heb. 1:3). With equal truth we can say that the individual Christian life begins with a man 'in Christ'—that is to say, when by faith we see ourselves seated together with Him in the heavens."[20]

spiritual word of God, even though the revelation be present in sight and sound. As a result of the fall his spirit is dead. The penitent who wills to accept the good news by faith is saved.[23] His spirit is quickened, and he sees that Jesus is Lord and surrenders himself. Later he familiarizes himself with the Bible and understands the full meaning of that single, basic revelation.

Nee formulates a second kind of revelation in the life of the minister of God's Word, the detailed revelation. Whereas the first kind (basic) is once for all at our rebirth, the second (detailed) is given time and again. In fact, every occasion wherein the Word is to be ministered must also be the occasion for a fresh revelation according to God's past revelations. For just as the New Testament is based upon the Old Testament revelation, so also the continuing revelation to the church is based on the Scripture and the initial revelation of Jesus as Lord. In a sense Nee appears to see the first revelation as God's gracious Word for the unbeliever, the second as His gracious Word in and through the believer.

Nee depicts revelation as coming to the believer as light.[24] Whether it comes to us in our drawing near to Jesus in prayer, through the ministry of others or indirectly in studying the Bible diligently, the light swiftly passes.[25] Light easily fades away from our memory. The greater the light to us the more difficult it is for us to remember. "Many brothers," Nee says, "confess that it is extremely difficult to remember the things they have read of spiritual revelation."[26] The light of revelation shines into the human heart, but God intends it to reach our human understanding (the mind).[27] Indeed this is, as Nee sees it, the problem with tongues without interpretation in 1 Cor. 14.[28] While tongues may be a valid expression of the onset of the divine light, Nee interprets verse 19 as requiring understanding for the ministry (or instructing) of the revelation to others. Nee goes on to describe the role of thought and understanding as one of "fixing" or "anchoring" the light. Without our understanding we cannot know its content nor claim the revelation in our spirit as ours.

In the Old Testament ministry it was not necessary for God to use the mind or understanding. Now with the full revelation of Christ's victory over death and His ascension as its antecedents, the New Testament ministry must also minister the same victory and power over the flesh, by God dealing with us.[29] In the language and style of Nee, "the outward man needs to be broken."[30] In brokenness God examines us and gives us knowledge of our human weaknesses. When God begins to deal with these weaknesses by His power, the broken man becomes rich in His thoughts. In Nee's study on ministry, *The Ministry of God's Word,* there is no single issue more important to him than brokenness. When the outward man is broken, all man's understanding and thought becomes subservient to whatever light is received by the spirit, and he lives as a spiritual man.

The divine, detailed revelation and the subsequent human, inner thought are not in themselves the message. But they are the essential components of what Nee identifies with the Old Testament prophet's usage of the term *massa.*[31] As the word denotes, revelation and thought become a psychokinetic weight upon the spiritual man.

In order to discharge his burden, the minister must seek for the "inner words" or word from God to give oral content to what is as yet inexpressible or ecstatic.

Further defined, the word within is in summary the divinely chosen message for a specific gospel presentation. Strictly conforming to the content of Scripture, it may come as a single word or as many as ten or so sentences. This word, for example, may be "For by grace have ye been saved through faith" (Eph. 2:8). Here it comes as a complete theological statement, but the listener is left with too many unanswered questions: Why has God reminded us of this now? What is the relationship between faith and grace? Is the emphasis of the minister's burden upon "grace," "faith" or "saved"? For according to Nee, the content is too strong and concentrated to be fully understood and digested by the listener.[32]

The inner word given by the Holy Spirit must now be translated or expanded into the "outer words" of human understanding and experiences. This transaction of the divine word is contingent upon the minister's own experience in Christian discipleship. If the minister's experience includes the breaking of the outward man, his words will be spiritual, accurate, of high quality and "touching" God. Without this experience he is unfit to preach, and his message, while outwardly clever and persuasive, is inwardly immature and unspiritual. The Apostle Paul represents the ideal example. For in 1 Corinthians 7 he speaks without special revelation, yet, he speaks God's Word.[33] For with Paul, as with the contemporary spiritual man, the outer words are created through brokenness in discipline and chastisement, not through purely human abilities. In the continual breaking of the outward man unto perfection the minister is most successful in distilling the ABCs of saving faith according to the needs and problems of the church and its witness to the world.

The Word Ministered

Nee describes two additional aspects that come into play as the outward word is being presented: memory and feelings.

Some of us by nature have good memories, and Nee believes such abilities can be a real advantage in recalling the inner word. Yet this outward memory too often fails or alters the word as it is delivered. God provides for the mnemonically weak a "Holy Spirit memory"[34] that recalls the spirit or pictures the inner words of revelation.

In the ministry right feelings must accompany the right words. In order for feelings, "the most delicate part in us,"[35] to be proper, Nee also sees the need for the outward man to be broken. If it is broken, the minister has only the strength of the inner man to rely on.

Trained to speak God's word, the minister must be willing to minister. He must, as Nee says, be willing to "push your spirit out, else the word will suffer greatly."[36] By this metaphysical push, the spirit is exercised and pours forth from life. While the experience may be quite exhausting,[37] this release of the spirit in ministry is a release of God's power, life and light to others.

Nee concludes his study of the ministry by offering some helps to speaking and a brief discussion of the audience of the word.[38] His helps contain no suggestions on homiletical style or technique, for Nee considers such instruction as an encouragement towards preaching by the soul and an assault on the primacy of the spirit. Rather he is concerned to "keep the spirit from being wounded,"[39] through contact with sin(s) or any imperfections of the incarnational dynamics of the word encountered by the minister. In the closing chapter, entitled "The Objects of the Word," Nee concedes that the congregation must also be spiritually attuned to receive spiritual things and can affect the delivery of the word. To the wise and intelligent (Matt. 11:25; 1 Cor. 1:19), the hard-hearted (Matt. 13:15) and those who blaspheme the Holy Spirit "God is unwilling to reveal himself, therefore He hides from them."[40] Under these circumstances the minister is hindered in his effort to release the Spirit, and his words suffer.

Conclusion

An essential feature in Nee's theology of the Word is his inflexible belief that God has not failed in the performance of His will. Part of that will is God's wish to use man:

> Man was created for God's specific purpose. As He did not make an obedient machine at the time of creation, so He now rejects the use of a preaching machine. He does not want an automaton; He wants a man with free will. It is a calculated risk with God to choose man as a minister of His word. Yet in spite of the complexity of man and his many problems such as sin, defilement, weakness, the outward man, and natural resistance, God still entrusts His word to man. Through the greatest rigor God obtains His highest glory.[41]

In that "calculated risk" both perfect love and man's natural potential to abrogate and eclipse the truth with himself become salient features of biblical and church history. And Watchman Nee understands his service to God in that history is to instruct in the way of the spiritual man, who administers truth.

Nee therefore places great emphasis on understanding the way in which the Holy Spirit overcomes the fallen nature to perfectly reveal the truth. This overcoming process of the Christian to permit perfect revelation in the church is summarized in the following illustration:

Stages in the Development of the Apostolic Ministry of the Word

THE REVELATION OF GOD

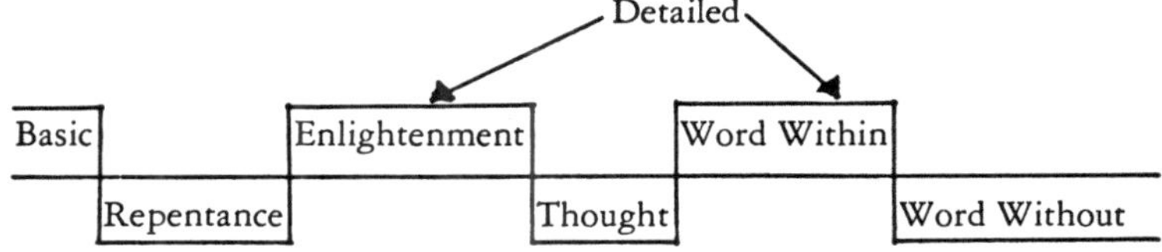

THE BREAKING OF THE OUTWARD MAN
IN THE MIND, EMOTIONS AND WILL
(The Preparation of the Man)

(Basic + Repentance = Conversion; Enlightenment + Thought = Burden)

While the church has no control over the content of God's sovereign revelation, it is responsible for the presentation and delivery of the message in its individual dealing with the outward man. In his own anthropological style Nee offers the instruction that the clear revelation enters into the life of the community through the spiritual man. While there may be much truth in Nee's statements that dedicated Christians (spiritual men) are better able to minister the Word of God than a scholarly elite,* Nee and his followers are always precariously close to a gnostic idea of the church. In such a church setting membership is not based on salvation in the person of Christ alone but on the knowledge of spiritual realities. Witness Lee himself has condemned Christendom for not accepting all of Nee's and Lee's "recovered" truths.[42]

---

*At least that is one way of interpreting the current rise of the evangelical church. They are better able to communicate to the mind and the needs of the laymen.

Anthropology:
The Spiritual Man and His Life

C. Ryder Smith, in his book *The Biblical Doctrine of Man,* reconstructs a biblical theology of man according to the New and Old Testaments' response to two paramount questions: "What is a man?" and "What ought a man to be?"[1] It is the latter question which becomes the central theme of all of Watchman Nee's writings. For he hypothesizes that the ills of the church can be traced to its failure to correctly answer this anthropological/theological question. From the beginning of his ministry he considered it his special task "to give God's children a clear understanding of spiritual life in order that the Holy Spirit might use it [*The Spiritual Man*] in leading the saints onward and in delivering them from groping in darkness."[2] While his multivolume work, *The Spiritual Man,* is the single most comprehensive statement of his doctrine of man, *Spiritual Reality or Obsession, The Latent Power of the Soul, The Release of the Spirit* and *The Normal Christian Life* are equally important studies on anthropology. The content of this chapter will deal with the specific principles developed in these five works.

The Trinity of Man
Theological speculation within the church on the

constitutional nature of man has divided into two lines of thought. Trichotomists hold that man is the unity of the human spirit (*ruach/pneuma*), soul (*nephesh/psuchē*) and body (*beten, geviyyah/sōma*). The dichotomists affirm the presence of an immaterial nature comprising both soul and spirit that reposes in the material element of the body of flesh. In the patristic age support was divided[3] on this as they attempted to theologize on the origin of the soul, the nature of immortality and the resurrection and the problem of sin in the life of the believer. While the Western Church has historically supported the dichotomous view, some have doubted whether this view is entirely applicable to the dynamics of the Christian life.

The critical, scientific age of the post-Reformation era presented new problems that required a further examination of the biblical perception of the human framework. William Harvey's study of the human heart (1616) revealed that this organ was a pump and not the seat of the human will. The heart and the entire body could therefore be examined and "healed" by the nonspiritual eye of the lay physician. James G. Frazer's study of comparative religion and culture, Franz Anton Mesmer's discovery of "personal magnetism," Freudian psychology and the parallel rise of the "Higher Life" Movement[4] created an intellectual climate suitable for a reworking of historical trichotomy and its intrapsychic dynamics.

Prior to his period, for example, the dichotomous approach had interpreted "spiritual warfare" as a battle between the flight of the soul to God and the inordinate passions of the human body. But the new trichotomy, far less cosmologically dualistic, concerned itself with the spiritual battle described in the Keswick interpretation of Rom. 5:12-8:17.[5] Here the presence of the "double I" in 7:14-25 and the contrast between the mind set on things of the flesh and the mind set on things of the spirit necessitated a more distinct, trichotomous bifurcation of the nonphysical elements of man. This rediscovery and reinterpretation of the tripartite construction of man is most apparent in the writings of J.B. Heard, Mary E. McDonough, Andrew Murray, G.H. Pember, Jessie Penn-Lewis, A.T. Pierson and Watchman Nee.[6]

At the very beginning of Watchman Nee's book *The Spiritual Man* he patently expresses his full support for a trichotomous position:

> The ordinary concept of the constitution of human beings is dualistic—soul and body. According to this concept soul is the invisible inner spiritual part, while body is the visible outer corporal part. Though there is some truth to this, it is nevertheless inaccurate. Such an opinion comes from fallen man, not from God; apart from God's revelation, no concept is dependable. That the body is man's outward sheath is undoubtedly correct, but the Bible never confuses spirit and soul as though they are the same. Not only are they different in terms; their very nature differs from each other. The Word of God does not divide man into two parts of soul and body. It treats man, rather, as tripartite—spirit, soul and body. 1 Thessalonians 5:23 reads: "May the God of peace himself sanctify you wholly; and may your spirit and soul and body be kept sound and blameless at the coming of our Lord Jesus Christ." This verse precisely shows that the whole man is

divided into three parts.[7]*

Nee goes on by saying that the dividing of soul and spirit is of "supreme importance,"[8] to spiritual growth and maturity. In Heb. 4:12 he sees the Word of God dividing our soul from our spirit. Analogous with the temple sacrifice that is divided by the priest's sword, Jesus divides us into three parts as the believer offers himself upon the altar of God.[9]

The Creation and Fall of Man

In most theologies that attempt to vindicate a three-part description of man, the Adamic creation account in Gen. 2:7 appears as a central text.[10] Watchman Nee is no exception.[11] Quite consistent with other trichotomous writers of his age, Nee sees the prefallen Adamic nature as a merging of spirit and body to form a third part—the human soul. While the angels are called "spirits," and animals have souls and bodies, only man is made in the tridimensional image of God: "A complete man is a trinity—the composite of spirit, soul and body."[12]

Somewhat like the divine trinity, Nee ascribes a specific function for each human part.[13] The corporal body is most clearly aligned to material reality and gives man his "world-consciousness." The soul, with its intellect and emotions, "belongs to man's own self and reveals his personality. It is termed as the part with 'self-consciousness.' "[14] The spirit apprehends, communes with and

---

*Here his concern is not so much with those who see the spirit as a functionally distinct unit, equal to the mind or heart, within the soul. Rather, Nee objects to a dualism which considers spirit and soul as synonymous with the human psyche. See pp. 98ff., "The Soul."

worships God and is the element of "God-consciousness." Taking his cue from Scripture references on an "inner" and "outward" man,[15] the three elements in his personality theory can be accurately depicted in this way:

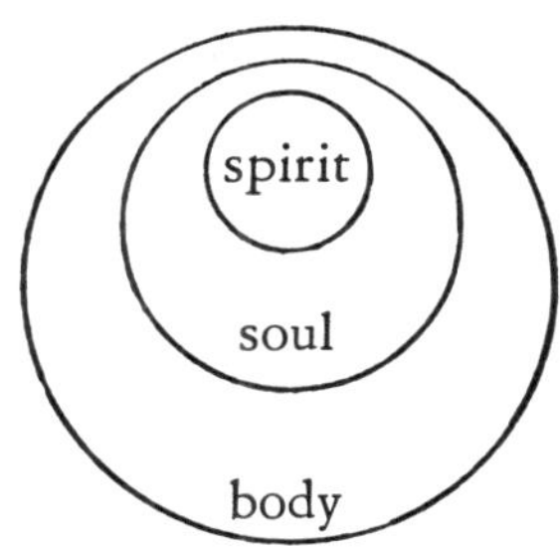

In this model it is clear that the soul occupies an important mediating position in determing whether Adam's outward actions conform to the inner witness of God's spirit.

As the product of the corporal and pneumatic union, the human soul is superior to the animal soul. It is the organ of man's free will, wherein his full potential as a servant of God or a doer of evil is realized. Before the fall, the soul was a steward of the spirit and could have become morally and spiritually in the image and likeness of God. On the basis of an apparent delegation of authority in Gen. 1:27-28, Nee believes Adam's soul was given tremendous power:

> Although we may not rate Adam's power as being a *billion* times over ours, we can nonetheless safely reckon it to be a *million* times over ours. Else he would have not

been able to perform the duty commanded him of God. As for us today, though, if we were required to merely sweep a lane three times daily, we would not be able afterwards to straighten our back. How then could we possibly rule the earth? Yet Adam not only ruled the earth but he also had dominion over the fish of the sea, the birds of the heavens, and every living thing on earth. To rule is not just to sit by doing nothing. It requires management and work. From a seeing of this we should recognize the superior power which Adam in fact possessed. It far exceeds our present situation.[17]

The body was likewise bestowed with immortality, incorruptibility and perfect health upon the condition of his obedience to God. His spirit and soul would then maintain the body in its created state forever without change.[18]

Each part of man was tremendously endowed by God and as such followed a proper hierarchy according to the Creator's will. The spirit was given the highest part of man's being, to which soul and body were subject:

> Under normal conditions the spirit is like a mistress, the soul like a steward, and the body like a servant. The mistress commits matters to the steward who in turn commands the servant to carry them out. The mistress gives orders privately to the steward; the steward in turn transmits them openly to the servant. The steward appears to be Lord of all, but in actuality the Lord over all is the mistress.[19]

In the Genesis narration two special trees have been set in the garden of Eden: the tree of life and the tree of the knowledge of good and evil. Nee sees in the two trees a "two-ways" tradition. The former germinates the way of the spirit, and the eating of its fruit is unrestricted. The latter develops the way of the soul, and its fruit is forbidden. At this point man was in a state of innocence and so to speak was "morally neutral—neither sinful nor holy."[20] Simultaneously he had the free will to assimilate either the fruit of spiritual life or the fruit of the soulical life. In a sense the two trees offered him a choice whether he would become a self-sufficient man, capable of deciding moral issues, or whether he would become dependent on God's judgment of right and wrong, partaking even of the life of God:

> Thus he would become a "son" of God, in the sense of having in him a life that derived from God. There you would have God's life in union with man: a race of men having the life of God in them and *living in constant dependence upon God for that life.* But if instead Adam should turn the other way, and take of the tree of the knowledge of good and evil, then he would develop his own manhood along natural lines apart from God. As a self-sufficient being, he would possess in himself the power to form independent judgment, *but he would have no life in God.*[21]

The history of mankind has shown the outcome of that choice. Apart from grace humanity is self-dependent, judging and acting without God. The serpent offered Adam greater power of the soul/self-consciousness through the knowledge of good and evil. In so doing Adam believed that the chasm between God's power and his own soul power could be breeched and he could be as a god.

In the fall* Adam disobeyed God's loving admonition, and this sin separated him from God's presence. The proper order of the human trilogy is disturbed. The soul ceases to be a steward of the spirit, and its power is "frozen" or immobilized. The soul is now puffed-up intellectually† to the degree that the spirit is deflated to the point of becoming dead in its sensitivity and activity toward God (Gen. 2:17).[24] Adam's body, barred from the tree of life and an immortal life with God, bears the mark of mortality, suffers pain and sickness and is under the reign of sin.

By the original sin all humanity suffers and must await the restoration through Christ, the second Adam. Original sin is our inheritance at birth and is a life of the soul marked by the dominion of the flesh. Such a life is centered on and often succumbs to the carnal needs of the body. Apart from the revelation of the law the unregenerate is even unconscious of being utterly sinful and corrupt.[25] His power and strength is not from God as received through the human spirit, but from the fallen soulical nature, devoid of any spiritual sense.

As prince of this world, it is the devil's intent to accuse and stir up this independent power. His purpose is to gain further control over man. Nee is convinced that this fallen and independent power of man provides much of the metaphysical dynamics of religious obsessions, cults, heresies and other religions.

---

*Nee also describes the temptation of Eve as an attack, first upon the needs of the body (eat), then of the soul (knowledge) and finally reaching her spirit (open rebellion against God).[22]

†"Because the fall of man was occasioned by seeking knowledge, God uses the foolishness of the cross to 'destroy the wisdom of the wise.' "[23]

Regardless of the unregenerate state of even the prophets,* God has fashioned the Old Testament revelation in such a way as to reveal the proper order of human nature: spirit, soul and body. In addition to Gen. 2:7, Nee lists a number of Old Testament passages in which he sees a scission in the role of the spirit and the role of the soul.[26] Nee is at least aware of the criticism that other passages† suggest that the Hebrew term for "soul" and "spirit" are synonymous. He concludes that the Old Testament disparity of the evidence also reveals that the unregenerate spirit, under the dominion of sin and death, functions semantically like the overpowering soul. "Before the believer is born again," Nee retorts, "his spirit becomes so sunken and surrounded by his soul that it is impossible for him to distinguish whether something is emanating from the soul or from the spirit."[28]

Even the Christian, due to long years of "soulical" bondage, knows very little of his spirit and must seek teaching through revelation and experience of what is soulish and what is spiritual. Nee feels it to be his ministry to recover this truth for the churches of God.[29]

An important Old Testament image for a tripartite humanity is found in the design of the temple. Taking Paul's comment in 1 Cor. 3:16 as a hermeneutical base, Nee sees direct functional relationships between the body and the outer court, the soul and the Holy Place, and the spirit and the Holy of Holies.[30] Like the body, the outer court is the place of external worship, and its life is

---

*See pp. 61-62, 69.

†Particularly, Gen. 41:8; Judg. 8:3; Prov. 14:29; 17:22; Isa. 29:24; 65:14; Dan. 5:20.[27]

visible to all. In the Holy Place the priest presents himself and his offering to God. Similarly the soul is the inner life of man, where he may offer up his emotions, volition and mind to God. The Holy of Holies is the dwelling place of God and cannot be reached by man unless the veil is rent. Its purpose parallels that of the spirit, where man unites and communes with God.

Christ: The Sum of All Spiritual Things

While the Old Covenant was set in the economy/dispensation of the law and the promise, it is in the New Covenant of Christ's ministry that the restoration to completeness of spiritual life begins and ends. Christ is the promised redeemer. For, as a result of the sin that permeates spirit, soul and body, the spiritual death that has separated man from God has spread to all men. No self-improvement theology of salvation can change this:

> Death has permeated the spirit, soul and body of all men; there is no part of a human being into which it has not found its way. It is therefore imperative that man receive God's life. The way of salvation cannot be in human reform, for "death" is irreparable. Sin must be judged before there can be rescue out of death.[31]

Since sin has wrought death to the entire man, Christ's atonement through death is a death through His entire triune nature.[32] His physical suffering atoned for sins conducted by the body. By refusing a sedative (wine mingled with myrrh), *He also refused to lose conscious-

---

*There is some debate whether the "wine mingled with myrrh" mentioned in Mark 15:23 is a sedative or a local beverage. See n. 33.

ness, to atone for the will in man's soul. In many ways He had been humiliated and thereby further atoned for man's soul. But His greatest suffering was spiritual in that He was abandoned by God (cf. Matt. 27:46).

In a number of references Nee speaks of the believer's identification with Christ's death, and His death is reckoned as our death.[34] From that point on, the work of translating man into the image of God can begin. At the same time that he has died with Christ, the believer is raised into newness of life and receives a new human spirit from God. As the temple needs the Holy of Holies to be the tabernacle or dwelling place of God, so also man receives a new spirit that becomes a dwelling place of God's Spirit.

Unlike Andrew Murray, Nee preached that the reception of the Holy Spirit is not experienced in a second work of grace but is part of the believer's initial salvation event.[35] But like many expositors of the Pentecostal or Holiness doctrines on the Spirit, Nee felt that conversion is not the only experience in what he calls "the normal Christian life." Four experiences are listed and described, each of which begins with a further, "objective," revelation of Christ and the cross.[36]* For each stage is only a further realization of the depth of human weakness and of the depth and scope of our need of union and identification in the death and resurrection of Christ:

> What we need to comprehend before God is that our experience there is neither thing nor affair but only Christ: not that He gives us light, but that He *is* our light;

---

*See pp. 107-123 in this chapter.

not that He leads the way, but He *is* the way; not that He gives us a life, but He *is* our life; not that He teaches a truth, but He *is* truth. Brethren, do you grasp the difference here? Whatever Christ gives is His very own self.[37]

Every enlightenment starts with more knowledge of Christ, because "God's Christ is all things; aside from Him God has nothing."[38] The four experiences are "justification and the new birth," "deliverance from sin," "the gift of the Holy Spirit" and "pleasing God." Subjectively, each serves as a further step in the believer's walk with the Lord, both as a crisis and a process of growth.

The importance of this growth process in Nee's theology has thus far been overlooked. Yet the steps comprise much of the meaning and content of *The Spiritual Man* and *The Normal Christian Life*. In the former Nee describes Christian growth in terms of his tripartite formula of spirit, soul and body. In the latter, produced some ten years later, growth structure is presented in terms of the Keswick interpretation of Roman 5-8 and the work of the cross. In both the basic purpose or aim of the message is to provide guidance for those who wish to be "overcomers" of the world and their fallen human natures. It is nothing less than the victorious Christian life.

At the very base of these four graces of spiritual life is his detailed understanding of the tripartite being. For every work of the cross in the life of the believer strengthens or counteracts some aspect or characteristic of the spirit, soul or body that hinders the effectual implementation of the Christian walk with God. Because of the extent of the reconstruction of man, two works of grace are not enough; four responses to revelation are necessary. The rest of this chapter will first look at Nee's descriptive profile of the inner workings of man and then will examine how they are affected by Nee's four works of grace.

Spirit

One of the fundamental principles of Watchman Nee's theology is that the spirit is the place where the regenerated man works together with God.[39] Within his regenerated spirit lie all the works of God towards him, and he must not mistake its activity with that of the soul's. The Holy Spirit resides there and first reveals and applies the finished work of the cross to the believer. As he states, "God's aim in a regenerated man is for that man by his spirit to rid himself of everything belonging to the old creation, because within his regenerated spirit lie all the works of God towards him."[40]

As the organ of God-consciousness, the Christian must realize he has a spirit. If he does, he can understand the meaning of the cross, resist the flesh and pray "with all perseverance until the answer comes."[41] His service to God will neither be subject to his emotions, nor by the cleverness of his mind, nor by the strength of his will, but by the will of God. If he is unconscious of his own spirit and its activities, his spirit may become defiled, and his ministry will not honor and glorify the Lord.

In addition to realizing that we have a spirit, Nee is concerned that the believer should understand and assimilate the laws of the spirit that are necessary for the spiritual walk. Knowledge of these laws comes only as one gets acquainted with the different functions that are distinctive to the spirit's work.[42] In his analysis of the spirit he lists three main functions: intuition, communion and conscience. In keeping with his typological emphasis, Nee metaphorically compares these functions with the Ark of the Covenant in the Holy of Holies.[43] Within the ark lies the law of God; by the spirit's intuition God makes his will and himself known. The mercy seat upon the ark manifests God's glory and receives a worship offering of blood; in communion man's blood-cleansed spirit worships and converses with the living God. The ark is the "Ark of Testimony" in that the two tablets of the law silently accused or excused Israel's actions; the believer's conscience also bears witness for or against his conduct.

Intuition

"Intuition" serves as the sense organ of the spirit, for it responds directly to the things beyond human understanding or cause.* Contrary to all rational and discernible evidence the intuition may speak out with "an unuttered and soundless voice" strongly opposing decisions conceived by the outward man. Nee is concerned that the believer be diligent to distinguish the inner voice from any outer feelings.

Intuition receives the anointing that teaches:

---

*Nee cites the following biblical texts as evidence of the human intuition: Matt. 26:41; Mark 2:8; 8:12; Luke 1:47; John 4:23; 11:33; 13:21; Acts 17:16; 18:25; 19:21; 20:22; Rom. 12:11; 1 Cor. 2:11; 14:15-16; 2 Cor. 2:13; 4:13; Eph. 1:17; Col. 1:8.[44]

You have been anointed by the Holy One, and you all
know. . . . But the anointing which you received from
him abides in you, and you have no need that any one
should teach you; as his anointing teaches you about
everything, and is true, and is no lie, just as it has taught
you, abide in him.[45]

This "anointing" brings us into a sense of knowledge of spiritual things. It is not the same thing as a mental understanding, and Nee is quick to point out the difference and division of the two. Human understanding rests upon intellectual accomplishment, whereas "knowing" by the spirit is a nonrational assurance in matters of faith that cannot be directly communicated to others.

One of the ways in which this "anointing of the spirit" helps is in the area of discerning the truth from lies and "what is of Christ from what is of the antichrists."[46] Without discernment, Nee concludes, only a Christian with a good mind and education would escape deception. While Nee nowhere suggests that the Christian faith is irrational or logically inconsistent with itself, he does feel that the believer's first bulwark against deception is the intuitive "small voice."[47]

In dealing with people the Christian's spirit can give unmistakable discernment about certain individuals. Investigation through inquiry and observation can occupy only a second place in understanding people. Such methods are insensitive to the human heart and therefore cannot be used as the primary tool to evaluate people. As an example of such intuitive understanding, Nee remarks on a child's gift in accurately understanding people and Jesus' discernment of the scribes in Mark 2:8. Such childlikeness and Christlikeness, Nee remarks, "ought to be the normal condition of every spiritual person."[48]

In the previous chapter of this book, dealing with "The Word and Its Ministry," it was noted that Nee believed in the continuing revelation in the man who has received the basic revelation/light of salvation.[49] It is in his intuition that man receives that light:

> To know things in our intuition is what the Bible calls revelation. Revelation has no other meaning than that the Holy Spirit enables a believer to apprehend a particular matter by indicating the reality of it to his spirit. There is but one kind of knowledge concerning either the Bible or God which is valuable, and that is the truth revealed to our spirit by God's spirit.[50]

He is quick to add that it must be distinguished or divided from certain special experiences or intellectual comprehension:

> This kind of revelation is not a vision, a heavenly voice, a dream, or an external force which shakes the man. One may encounter these phenomena and still not have revelation. Revelation happens in the intuition—quietly, neither hastily nor slowly, soundless and yet with a message. How many denominate themselves Christians, though the Christianity they embrace is simply a kind of philosophy of life or of ethics, a few articles of truth, or some supernatural manifestations. Such an attitude will neither issue in a new birth nor a new spirit. Numerous are these "Christians" whose spiritual usefulness measures up to zero. Not so are those who have received Christ, for by the grace of God they have perceived in their spirit the reality of the spiritual realm, which opens to them like

the lifting of a veil. What they today *know* is far more profound than what their mind has comprehended; yea, it seems as though a new meaning has been imparted to all which they had only understood or comprehended in the past.[51]

Since the believer's life is characterized by two-way communication, there are two kinds of revelation in our spirit: the direct and the sought. In direct revelation God has a particular wish for the believer and reveals it through a regenerate spirit. In "sought revelation" the less mature believer seeks an answer to a specific need and awaits an answer through God's movement in his spirit.[52] The sum total of both kinds of revelation received within the individual's spirit is the entire content of his spiritual knowledge.[53] Nee warns that no amount or argument, reason or contemplation can add to it. Although the mind has value secondarily, any experience arising out of it is from man himself and does not come through intuition, man's spiritual sense organ.

Communion

The second function of the spirit is communion. As defined in the second volume of *The Spiritual Man*, it is not at first apparent whether a real distinction exists between intuition and communion. Nee even begins his analysis of communion by identifying it as an intuitive faculty. But as further defined, communion is the activity of receiving the revelation of God through one's intuition.[54] If the Christian remains spiritual, his intuition is alive, and he will enjoy uninterrupted communion with God. Worship does enter into the communion relationship, but Nee's emphasis is more towards communion as apprehension of spiritual knowledge and understanding. He seems to steer clear of any type of balanced presentation of an I-Thou understanding of communion. For the believer to speak his mind in prayer is considered rather superficial and immature by Nee.[55] Christians are rather to set their worship to the cognition of the mind of God:

> Many devotional prayers, prayers of fellowship, and prayers of request cannot be a substitute for prayer as ministry or work. If all our prayers are simply devotional or merely consist of fellowshipping and asking, our prayer is *too small.* Prayer as work or ministry means that we stand on God's side, desiring what He desires. To pray according to God's will is a most powerful thing. For the church to pray signifies that she has discovered God's will and is now voicing it. Prayer is not only asking God, it is also the making of a declaration. As the church prays, she stands on God's side and declares that what man wants is what He wants. If the church should so declare, the declaration will be at once effectual. (Italics mine.)[56]*

Any prayer that does come from the mind (1 Cor. 14:15) must have its content originate from the revelation of the spirit.

Conscience

The final function of the spirit, conscience, corrects and reprimands when men fall short of the glory of God. It expresses the holiness of God and is extremely important in the life of the believer and nonbeliever as

---

*Nee appears to have modified his stand near the end of his ministry. See *Living Sacrifice,* pp. 82-97.

well. While the unbeliever's spirit is dead, the death of the conscience is not as deep as that of communion. Hence the conscience can arise out of its comatose state to accuse even the unregenerate. But without communion with God his conscience cannot reveal the eternal, spiritual life to him.[57]

For a believer has been quickened at his rebirth, and he is consequently more sensitive to sin. Once he transgresses God's ordinances, the conscience immediately testifies that he is not clear towards God and towards men. Invariably the believer will repent or quench its protest by arguing or trying to appease it with a show of good works.[58]

The spiritual man hears the voice of conscience and allows the Holy Spirit to point out every one of his sins. Confessing his sins, he trusts in the precious blood of Christ for cleansing and continually seeks the will of God in his life. Inseparable from his great faith he has a good conscience (cf. 1 Tim. 1:5, 19) and therefore can freely converse with God.[59] Finally his conscience assures him that as far as his spiritual knowledge goes he has arrived at the immediate goal of perfection, a foretaste of his eschatological completion in the resurrection.*

A believer with a weak conscience has a different ethic by which to live than a man with a good conscience.[61] The freedom in Christ of a believer with a weak conscience is limited according to the level of grace he has thus far experienced in his life. While another man may have a clear conscience to eat meat offered to idols (as in

---

*Like Wesley, Nee seems to be making a distinction between deliberate and indeliberate sins.[60]

1 Cor. 8-10), his conscience is disturbed. He has not yet come to know the full meaning of the cross and his liberty in the New Covenant. To go against his conscience now would be for him and for God an act of willful disobedience.

In his analysis Nee stresses the point that all three functions of the spirit are "intertwined."[62] As such it is essential to the life of the spirit that each function should be carried out according to the work of the Holy Spirit. If one function is hindered or suffers, the entire spirit is affected.

Laws of the Spirit

Once the believer understands that his spirit must be intuitively open to revelation, be in communion with God and have a clear conscience, he can appreciate the laws of the spirit. Nee lists eight laws of the spirit (italics added):

1) *The spirit needs to be kept in a state of perfect freedom.*[63] The believer may often sense oppression and heaviness weighing upon his spiritual life. Nee warns that such a sensation is an attack of Satan to dull his spiritual sense to the degree that it hinders the work of God. If encountered in the morning, the whole day will be a loss to him and to the church. Nee admonishes the church to deal with oppression of the spirit immediately:

> The way to handle it is to stop the work at hand at once, set your will against this weight, and exercise your spirit to oppose it. Occasionally you may have to utter words audibly against it; at other times with the power of your spirit you should resist in prayer.[64]

One must also attempt to uncover the cause behind his

oppression. Through spiritual discernment he will see some failure on his part to cooperate with God at a particular time with regard to a particular matter.

2) *The spirit requires the soul and body as the organ of its expression.*[65] In this maxim Nee states that one requirement for a normal expression of the spirit is a normal soul and body. When these parts cease to serve as the spirit's outlet, the believer loses his "aliveness," is bashful, and the public proclamation of his faith becomes hidden. Release comes through the exercise of his will in prayer and the declaration of the victorious name of the Lord Jesus over every onslaught of the enemy. Without his own prayers and the prayers of others he will continue to show the symptoms of spiritual suffocation until the outward man is broken.

3) *The spirit can be broken through sorrow, grief, anguish or heartbreak.*[66] Such emotions may not be elicited through the spirit and may be regarded as an attack of Satan. Such attacks of depression can create in us a number of abnormal symptoms. The Christian may become stiff, unyielding, narrow and selfish. Under his personality the whole church may become just as unforgiving, sectarian and prideful as he is. The poisoning of his spirit colors his speaking and must be dealt with quickly:

> The moment we notice our voice has turned harsh, we must stop instantly. With not the slightest hesitation we should turn to ourselves and say, "I am willing to speak with a pure spirit; I am willing to oppose the enemy." If we are reluctant to say to our brethren, "I am wrong," then our spirit remains engulfed in its sin.[67]

As a preventive, Nee encourages the believer to recognize faith as a shield against these "darts" of Satan.[68]

4) *The spirit "sinking or being submerged" into the soul is largely due to a turning in on oneself.*[69] Nee provides four symptoms of this "sinking" of the spirit. If he is possessive over all his spiritual experiences, if he has an intrusion of the power of darkness in his life, if his prayer and worship is self-centered or if he dwells in "physical sensations and various wonderful experiences" supplied by Satan, his spirit is most certainly sinking.[70] If the sinking continues, Nee even says, "He may perhaps be possessed by the evil spirit." To prevent the spirit from any further sinking in the soul, the believer's spirit must flow out. Only when the spirit is directed outward can the believer's spirit be restored to its original state.

5) *"The burden of the spirit differs from the weights on the spirit."* The former issues from God, and the freedom of prayer is never lost; the latter is an oppression from Satan that inhibits prayer.[71]

6) *God's life and power in the spirit can recede like a tide.*[72] This law is a corollary to law number two. For the recession of God's life is not God's fault but the result of an obstructed outlet. The signs of this condition are given in some detail and appear to describe the actual experience of many believers:

> Day by day he grows weaker. At this time he seems to lose his taste for communion with God: his Bible reading becomes meaningless: rarely, if at all, is his heart touched by any message or special verse. Moreover, his prayer turns dry and dreary as if there is neither sense nor word;

and his witnessing appears to be forced and reluctant, not overflowing as before.[73]

Nee likens God's life in us to a river that does not subside but may cease to flow if hindered by the human flesh.

When God's life stops flowing, one must pray and meditate to find the reason that the Holy Spirit has ebbed in his life. While waiting upon God "he should try to unearth where he has failed to fulfill the condition for the steady flow of God."[74] In every case the problem is not God but the human flesh.

7) *Deprived of its normal condition, the spirit loses contact with the Holy Spirit and is sometimes darkened.*[75] If the person allows his spirit to be misguided in any way, he may become disconnected from the Holy Spirit and is sometimes darkened.[75] Nee exhorts the believer to keep his spirit in "a tender and pliable state."[76] Otherwise the Christian may come to have a "haughty spirit" (Prov. 16·18) or a spirit that has strayed off the course set by God.

8) *"A child of God ought to know what is and what is not the normal condition for his spirit."*[77] Nee classifies the spirit according to four conditions:

(a) The spirit is oppressed and is therefore in decline.
(b) The spirit is under compulsion and so is forced into inordinate activity.
(c) The spirit is defiled (2 Cor. 7:1) since it has yielded ground to sin.
(d) The spirit is quiet and firm because it occupies its rightful position.[78]

It is most important to what Nee calls "the walk of the spirit" that one's spirit be purified from the first three conditions. The spirit in its rightful place enables the flow of God to penetrate to the outward man, so that the work of God may be carried out in His church.

Whenever the laws of the spirit have been obeyed, the spirit reaches a state of "normalcy" and demonstrates certain virtues of the inner man. A normal spirit is humble and contrite (Isa. 57:15), gentle and quiet (1 Pet. 3:4), poor and yet joyful, strong and yet broken, fervent and yet cool. The spirit responds appropriately to the given circumstances. "We must have a spirit of power towards the enemy," Nee says, "a spirit of love towards men, and a spirit of self-control towards ourselves."[79] And in spite of his extensive teaching on the nature of spiritual growth, Nee believes that a normal spirit does not pay a great deal of attention to, and reflection upon, his own spiritual growth. For Nee, "Full salvation delivers a believer out of himself and into God."[80]

In Nee's writings the human spirit serves as the essential medium between God's presence in the church through the Holy Spirit and man's human presence in the local congregation and the world.[81] Whether the spirit is able to convey what has been communicated or revealed, in large measure, depends upon the function and normalcy of the human soul, the second part of the human triplicity.

The Soul
The soul relates us to ourselves and gives man a sense of reflective awareness, which Nee calls self-conscious-

ness.* While he contends that it is the spirit that God is most concerned with, a greater portion of Nee's anthropological writings is concerned with the nature and operation of the soul. The reason is simple. As has been stated earlier, one of the primary concerns of Nee's ministry was the deliverance of the saints from darkness. The source of that darkness, as Nee interprets it, is the abnormality of the soul within the church.[82] God's desire is to see the soul perfected in its role as the medium through which the spirit can touch the body and thereby enable the spiritual world of revelation to reach the physical world that men communicate and live in. As God seeks to develop further the free functions of the spirit, Satan is active in strengthening the three parts of the human soul—emotion, mind and will—to establish "soulish or carnal Christians" who actively hinder the work of God.

Emotion

"Emotion may be denominated the most formidable enemy to the life of a spiritual Christian," Nee warns.[83] Far too often Christians have allowed their emotions to serve as the barometer of their faith. But the emotional life is one of vacillation and is entirely undependable:

> The emotion of man often displays a reactionary motion: a time of activity in one direction will sometimes produce an opposite reaction. For example, unspeakable sorrow usually follows upon hilarious joy, great depression after high excitement, deep withdrawal after burning fervor. Even in the matter of love, it may commence as

---

*See pp. 78ff.

such but due to some emotional alteration it may end up with a hatred whose intensity far exceeds the earlier love.[84]

Young Christians who have as yet not obtained a degree of fitness to receive daily spiritual guidance will invariably turn to their emotions. They are most probably the victims of ignorance and are in need of further teaching and counseling. Others who have walked for some time with Christ, "who have experienced the dividing of spirit and soul and who recognize the stirrings of emotion as being soulish and instantly resist can nonetheless walk after emotion."[85] Their demise is due to the success of some "spiritual" counterfeit by the emotion that outwardly appears to be from the spirit. For example, one may study psychology as a technique so that his words, teachings, presentations, manners and interpretations can be more psychologically appealing to those whom he wishes to win to Christ.[86] He does not, however, realize that such techniques do not win people to Christ; they only produce psychological conversions that will subside with an alteration of feelings. Such carnality of emotion can only be overcome by exercising the will to submit our emotions to the cross, so that they reflect only the feelings initiated by the spirit.

Affection is an aspect of our emotional life that can hinder the work of the spirit.[87] God demands that we love Him with all our heart, yet the natural man or carnal believer distributes his affection. Love of wife, children or friends is often set against one's love of God. Yet God desires that we consecrate our affections, so that we will love men—even God—with God's love.[88] Soulish love loves God for the pleasure of the emotion, is interested in the attractions of the world, alternates all too readily, is more active among friends of the opposite sex and fluctuates broadly according to one's emotions. Contrarily, love in a spiritual man is far above human natural affections and is guided by the spirit.[89]

"Desire occupies the largest part of our emotional life: it joins forces with our will to rebel against God's will."[90] Its influence is greater than mere love of pleasure; for it also includes pride, ambition, inordinate fascination with worldly things, self-justification and an impetuosity of the flesh that cannot wait upon God. It is God's aim and the experience of the spiritual man that one's desire should be crucified, not suppressed. Once man's desire is that of God's, then the believer finds the rest of a "satisfied life."[91]

The Mind

The mind, the second element of the soul, is extensively described and commented upon in both *The Spiritual Man* and *Spiritual Knowledge*. The latter treatise comes as a shift in Nee's opinion on the nature of the mind. In the former brain and mind are one; in the latter a tripartite division is made between the two components and human intuition:

> Now let us further say that man has three different organs for knowledge. In the body is the brain, in the spirit is the intuition, and in the soul is the nous [Greek for mind]. When we dissect the brain, we see nothing but the gray and white substance. And intuition is something which we sometimes sense and sometimes do not sense.

At times it seems to constrain, at other times it seems to restrain. It is that entity which is deep down in us. But the nous stands between the intuition and the brain. It interprets the meaning in the intuition and directs the brain to express it in words.[92]

While the ultimate meaning and interpretation that Nee ascribes to the mind has not shifted, the two books do point to the problem of Nee's attempt to parallel contemporary, postscientific knowledge with the prescientific world view of Scriptures.[93] Regardless of the truth of the Scriptures' human insights, the Bible does not equate or identify brain function with thought.[94] Nee, however, does attempt this, first through a holistic view, equating mind with brain; secondly, with a tripartite division of body (brain), soul (mind) and spirit (intuition).[95]

The mind of the unbeliever is blinded by Satan, corrupted and depraved (Rom. 1:28, 2 Tim. 3:8), futile and vain (Eph. 4:17), fleshly (Col. 2:18) and defiled (Titus 1:15).[96] Whenever the gospel message is presented to him, his mind invents a host of arguments and reasonings to keep himself from seeing the glory of Christ. At this point a battle rages that will be decided by the exercise of man's will:

Man's will and spirit are like a citadel which the evil spirits crave to capture. The open field where the battle is waged for the seizure of the citadel is man's mind. Note how Paul the Apostle describes it: "though we live in the world we are not carrying on a worldy war, for the weapons of our warfare are not wordly but have divine power to destroy strongholds. We destroy *arguments* and every proud obstacle to the knowledge of God, and take every *thought* captive to obey Christ" (2 Cor. 10:3-5). He initially tells of a battle—then where the battle is fought—and finally for what objective. This struggle pertains exclusively to man's mind.[97]

Once man's mind is captured by divine revelation, God's mighty power destroys his agnostic arguments by means of "repentance" (*metanoia* literally means "change of mind ").[98]

After regeneration the believer's mind is not liberated totally from Satanic activity and will continue to suffer the onslaught of Satan more than any other organ of the whole man. The mind is his weakest point. Since Satan has lost the first battle upon the believer's conversion, he now concentrates his effort on deceiving the mind with false teachings, prejudices and narrow-minded theories, opinions and objectives. "History is strewn with innumerable cases of sanctified saints who propagated heresies!" Nee contends.[99] While their hearts* may be in a state of active communication with God, they may unknowingly accept Satanic suggestions. Such believers who have not had their minds renewed in their Christian walk show their lack of common sense and practical wisdom by their outward actions. Neglecting the proper use of their minds, their thoughts are cluttered with a collage of diverse thoughts and worldly images.

Many other mental symptoms can be attributed to the work of the enemy and can be quite easily distinguished

---

*Nee defines "heart" as the "conscience" and the "mind." The heart acts as an exchange between the workings of the Spirit and soul: "The spirit reaches the soul via the heart; and through the heart the soul conveys to the spirit what it has gathered from outside."[100]

from spiritual insights. Unlike "normal" mental activity abnormal thoughts from Satan always appear without any conscious effort of the will.[101] The operating requirements of the Holy Spirit and of the evil spirit in the brain are also different:

(1) All supernatural revelations, visions or other strange occurrences which require *total cessation of the function of the mind,* or are obtained only after it has ceased working, are not of God.

(2) All visions which arise from the Holy Spirit are conferred when the believer's mind is fully active. It necessitates the active engagement of the various functions of the mind to apprehend these visions. The endeavors of evil spirits follow exactly the opposite course.

(3) All which flows from God agrees with God's nature and the Bible.[102]

Once a person is aware of this, he should exercise his will and resist the enemy with the power of Christ.

All too often the believer has let his mind be overrun with evil by giving ground to Satan in six different ways: (1) through an unrenewed mind that has not been consecrated to God; (2) through a mind that cherishes sin; (3) by misunderstanding God's truth and accepting a lie; (4) by accepting Satanic suggestions, particularly in discerning his circumstances and the future; (5) by allowing the mind to be blank and atrophied, out of a lack of proper mental experiences; and (6) by prayer done with a passive mind.[103]

Nee is particularly critical of popular philosophies and theologies that encourage a passivity of mind. Scientific hypnotism, yoga and even many teachings on the reception of the gift of tongues[104] instruct adherents to let their minds go free or become blank, and Nee believes this to be unbiblical. "By examining every instance in the New Testament where God's supernatural revelation is recounted," Nee states, "we find that everyone there who experiences a revelation does so with his mind functioning and with the ability *to control himself* and use any part of his body."[105] Many intellectual and psychological works of Satan, including false teachings, insomnia, forgetfulness, mental fatigue, theological vacillation, talkativeness and obstinacy, have entered into the life of the church and the life of the believer through a passive mind.

Once the mind has been renewed through the work of the cross, it acts as an auxiliary to the human spirit.[106] Whenever the spirit, for whatever reason, is not led to pray or does not deliver some needed guidance from the Holy Spirit, the mind exercises its understanding by actively praying. This is, at least, Nee's interpretation of "pray[ing] with the mind" in 1 Cor. 14:15.[107] In so doing, the mind of the soul is within the proper organismic relationship as a steward of the spirit.[108] Likewise the spirit receives knowledge intuitively but needs our mental faculties to understand its meaning. The mind also serves as the translator of truth received through the preaching of the Word by other members of the body of Christ. Finally, the mind is most able to serve the spirit when it is exercised in the systematic reading and memorization of God's Word.

The Will

According to God's plan in the Christian life, the will,

the third and final component of Nee's tripartite soul, ought to be in submission to the will of God.[109] Whether the will is in submission depends not upon an unconditional predetermination of God's elect, but rather upon the decision of "the sovereign, independent, free will of man."[110]* Nee clearly differs from the rigid "five-point" Calvinistic perspective, in that he affirms a universal atonement and that man's will plays an important part in the regenerative/sanctification process of the Christian life.

Still Nee does see the prodigious damage suffered by the human volition/will as a result of the fall. In the Garden of Eden, placed between the two massive contradictory wills of God and Satan, man chose to ignore the will of the Creator for the created, and his own will became captive and underwent corruption.[112] Without God's intervention in history all of mankind would remain fleshly, unable to save himself, perform any spiritual good or avoid sinning. On two different occasions Nee has compared John 1:13 and Rev. 22:17 and concluded that the only way to reconcile the two texts is to insist that the will is effectual unto salvation only because salvation commences with God. The will cannot save itself; it can only accept or reject God's salvation gift of love

---

*Nee goes on to say, "Though God is the Lord of the entire universe, yet He is willing to be restricted by a non-encroachment of man's free will. He never forces man to be loyal to Him. And Satan likewise is unable to usurp any part of man without the latter's *consent* granted either knowingly or unknowingly. Both God and the devil require man to be persuaded before operating in him. When man 'desires' good, God will accomplish it; but when he 'desires' evil, the wicked spirit will fulfill it. This is what we see in the Garden of Eden."[111]

toward him in the form of Jesus Christ.[113]

The importance of the will in carrying out God's purposes in man's life does not end with salvation. Every step of the Christian walk requires a surrender of our own wills and an absolute yielding to God's will. Many of God's children, Nee warns, will go through "various unpleasant strippings" in order that our wills may be proven faithful:

> He causes them to lose material things: health, fame, position, usefulness. What is more, He even causes them to be deprived of joyous feeling, burning desire, the presence and comfort of God. He must show them that everything except His will must be denied. If it is God's will, they should be willing to accept pain and suffering upon their physical bodies. They must be ready to embrace dryness, darkness and coldness if He seems pleased to so treat them. Even if He should so strip them of everything, of even so called spiritual effectiveness, they must accept it. He wishes His own to know that He saves them not for *their enjoyment* but for His Own will. In gain or loss, joy or sorrow, consciousness of His presence or that of His rejection, Christians must contemplate God's will alone.[114]

According to Nee, the intent of God here is twofold: He desires, first, that our wills obey Him and, secondly, that the "tendency" or "life" of the will that secretly awaits the opportunity to disobey be "smashed," broken and put to death. Through the working of the cross the believer will be both in obedience and in harmony with the universal will of God.

There are two dangerous attitudes which the believer must be aware of, so that he will not give ground in his will to evil spirits. Nee classifies these dangers as one of commission and one of omission; positive sins and negative sins:

> Positive sins are those which a person commits: his hands perform bad acts, his eyes see evil scenes, his ears hear wicked voices, and his mouth speaks unclean words. These render opportunity to evil spirits in varying degree to take hold of the hands, eyes, ears and mouth of the saint.[115]

Such actions of willful sinning are the enemy's strategy among the "heathen" and among carnal Christians. Among Christians desirous of growing in grace, deception is offered in the way of negation or passivity of the will. Nee quotes Jessie Penn-Lewis and defines passivity as "a cessation of the active exercise of the will in control over spirit, soul and body, or either, as may be the case."[116]

Passive-willed Christians falsely believe that only God will energize their works and that nothing will be done apart from God's will and plan. Yet inactivity of the will only leads to inactivity of action. Such people wait for some external force to move them. These external motivations usually arise from the "prince of this world" and enable Satan to use our God-given talents and charismatic gifts according to His will and plan. Eventually these people become entrenched in a life that feels happy only when it is forced to do something.[117]

The source of the problem is ignorance, experienced even by spiritual brethren. While their motive in seeking God's will in their lives may be entirely pure and spiritual, they do not understand that God does not want man to be ordered mechanically and unconsciously.[118] In their false rationality they consider themselves beyond deception because of their frequent spiritual experiences. In addition they no longer understand the means of keeping their minds open to knowledge received in the Bible, by watching and praying.

Passive wills may be the result of personal laziness, but most often it is the result of misunderstanding the content of Scripture. Some misconstrue Gal. 2:20 to connote spiritual life as a life of self-effacement, achieved through a loss of personality and an absence of volition and self-control, and demonstrated in automatic obedience to God.[119] Others view Phil. 2:13 as denying the need for our own readiness "To will and to work." Many other misconceptions arise, particularly out of ignorance of the work of the spirit in obedience (Acts 5:32), the ruling of our spirit, speaking (Matt. 10:20), guidance (Isa. 30:21), memory (John 14:26), love (Rom. 5:5), weakness and suffering (2 Cor. 12:10) and humility (2 Cor. 10:12ff.).[120] In every case Christians have assumed that these matters may be best governed by a passive will that unquestionably accepts whatever occurs to them.

Obviously the way of recovery from the negative and positive sins of the will is through the exercise of the human will according to the Scriptures. First, Nee says, we must obey God's will through our own willingness and through an openness to His revelation and strengthening. Secondly, we must resist the devil's will with all the strength of our spirit, soul and body.* Finally, one must

---

*The resistance of the saints, however, must include the acceptance of our mistakes. "The worst fallacy one can ever commit is to reckon oneself infallible."[121]

resolve to follow God's pathway to freedom through the further exercising of the human will in collaboration with the collective will of the saints.[122]

The Soul: Its Latent Power

"Today's situation is perilous," wrote Nee in 1933.[123] As his indigenous movement began to grow and spread through China, he became increasingly aware of what he regarded as counterfeit spirituality within and without the Christian church. Healings, tongues,* miracles, prophecy and meditation, he believed, were all being Satanically manifested to mislead those who sought the truth and power of God.[125] Within the framework of his tripartite anthropology, he propounded a vaccine and a remedy in the dividing and discerning of the power of the Spirit emanating from the human spirit and the latent power originating with the soul.[126]

While the power in man's soul was at one time intended to serve God, it has now been outlawed as an energy source unfit for the body of Christ.[127]† The tremendous soul power exercised by Adam to name and rule the earth has been subjugated and circumscribed by the flesh as a result of the fall. Originally in the "likeness" of God's power, it can easily manufacture gifts quite like those "of the Spirit." Such supernaturalism can even be produced by Christians if Satan sufficiently tempts them to labor, even for the church, independently of God. If, for

---

*Animistic practices in Nee's Fukien Province included the practice of spirit possession by a young medium or "tang-ki." In these possessions the medium shakes and "performs unintelligible 'gods' language."[124]

†As in the example of Jesus' life.

example, prayer is projected towards the sick person instead of towards God, that person will become oppressed by the psychic/soulical power and will become even sicker. Others may use hypnotic techniques, singing and novel Bible teaching to bring about certain results, but in every case the real fruit of the spiritual life will be altogether absent. Christians in such instances have preferred the supernatural things of the psychic world rather than the supranatural working of God within the church.

Nee criticizes non-Christian religions for practicing aesthetic principles that release the power of the soul through overcoming the flesh. Whenever such goals are carried out, supernatural powers become available, including healings, mind reading, predicting the future and piercing the unknown past. Quite deceptively, Satan, through these cults and religions, causes men to substitute God's salvation and life for psychic miracles; what is of the spirit for what is of the soul.

The Body

In *The Spiritual Man,* Watchman Nee's study on the human body is much briefer and less complex than his analysis of the soul and the spirit. The reason is simple. The physician and biologist use their physical senses, aided by scientific instruments, to observe and describe the functions and structure of the physical body. The soul and spirit are metaphysical elements and are beyond natural observation. Nee was neither a doctor nor a biologist and therefore did not attempt to write any "tripartite" description of the body, according to a series of interacting units, as he had done with spirit and the soul. The local churches had invested him with the job of metaphysician, and, using the historic tools of the "inspired" Scripture in conjunction with personal revelation, Nee felt confident enough in the position to propose a practical metaphysical map of the soul and the spirit. Conversely the body was the realm of the physician. Nee did, however, remark on such physical matters that pertain to spiritual life.

Using Rom. 8:11 as a text, Nee taught that the believer can have life in his mortal body prior to the resurrection of the dead.* In this life the nature of the body is not unchangeable, for the quality of the body can be quickened, as evident in two ways: "(1) He will restore us when we are sick and (2) He will preserve us if we are not sick."[129] In the first, God heals us so that the spiritual work of the church may not be hindered by any sickness. In the second, the body is preserved from the assault of any disease or infirmity in order that it may perform services within the larger body of Christ. While accepting the use of modern medical aids when justified,[130] Nee stressed that the believer also has the spiritual potential to overcome the forces of sickness that seek to hinder the work of God.

The essential requirement for the believer to have this "life" in his body is to live the obedient life of the spiritual man. The spiritual man acknowledges his inability to control his own health. He allows the Holy Spirit to make real the crucifixion of the deeds and sicknesses of the body:

---

*It is most likely that Paul is here referring to the final resurrection of the body, contra. Nee. See n. 128.

Only the Holy Spirit can take what the cross has accomplished and make the believers experience it. If we hear the truth of the cross but do not allow Him to work into our lives, then we know nothing but a theory and an ideal.[131]

Nee uses 1 Cor. 6:12-40, with its emphasis on the human body as members in the body of Christ, to support his belief that God desires the full deliverance of the body from fleshly needs, sin and physical ills. Through the medium of the Spirit we are healed by His stripes.[132] Under the governorship of the same Spirit the body of the spiritual man responds to its natural needs only insofar as it glorifies the Lord, not for the satisfaction of personal desires. Likewise, to sin against the body is to sin against Christ, for the body is God's temple.[133] In all, surrender to the work of the Holy Spirit is a necessary condition—the essence—of the spiritual man.

In the matter of sickness Nee gives extended comments upon the relationship between sin and sickness and between sickness and sanctification.[134] Sin is closely correlated with sickness in the life of the believer. Not in a negative sense—where sickness is regarded as punishment for unconfessed wickedness and vice—but in a positive way sickness is interpreted as an important opportunity for the faithful to perceive whether his life is centered on the self or upon the witness of the spirit:

> The heart of a believer is far from God's. God permits him to be ill that he may forget himself; but the more ill he grows the more self-loving he becomes; he endlessly dwells on his symptoms in his anxiety to find a cure. Almost all thoughts revolve about himself! How attentive he now is to his food, what he should or should not eat!

How worried he is when anything goes awry! He takes great care for his comforts and rest. He agonizes if he feels a bit hot or cold or has suffered a bad night, as though these were fatal to his life. How sensitive he is to the way people treat him: do they think enough of him, do they take good care of him, do they visit him as often as they should? Countless hours are exhausted in just this way of thinking about his body; and so he has no time to meditate on the Lord or on what the Lord may be wanting to accomplish in his life. Indeed, many are simply "bewitched" by their sickness! We never truly know how excessively much we love ourselves until we become sick![135]

Sickness is the result of the universal fall of man and therefore is a universal condition. No man, Christian or non-Christian alike, experiences perpetual perfect health. But individually, the believer must ask what is the reason for the sickness that has befallen him. Patiently the Christian should find God's purpose in allowing infirmity to fall upon him. Has some transgression gone unnoticed, has he defiled his body—the temple of God—or, more likely, is God further instructing him to deny self and to trust God and His spirit? Once the ill believer has settled this question, he can begin to recover. Trusting in God, he will no longer covet a cure through man's drugs but will abide by the spirit's leading. Recovery is inevitable according to the physical (medical) and spiritual means provided for by God. Only when "a Christian plainly knows his work is finished"[136] will the sickness end in death. Until that time death must be resisted by our abiding faith in the work of the cross.[137]

The Fourfold Work of the Cross

How does one appropriate the work of Christ? This question provides much of the conflict and dynamics of the extensive writings of Watchman Nee. Yet studies done by Erling, Kinnear, Henry and Lyall[138] have entirely ignored or seem unaware of this, the major input of his teachings. In *The Spiritual Man* and *The Normal Christian Life* the question of redemptive appropriation is presented in the form of a fourfold work of the cross upon the personhood and labors of the believer. Each of these phases of the cross has a specific pattern of revelation and then experience. Further, the experience "usually takes the two-fold form of a crisis leading to a continuous process."[139] The end result of this process is the spiritual man. And the ongoing life of the spiritual man is the normal Christian life.

The first two works of grace are concerned with the state of our being. The next two are concerned with the nature of our service. The order here of resolving the problems of being before the patterns of service are fashioned is most important. For all true service begins with the regenerated person whose soul submits to the spirit's intuition, communion and conscience and not with the unregenerate man whose soul rebels and succumbs to the passions of the body. All that an unregenerated person is, according to Nee, is "flesh." And once this flesh has been dealt with, the believer can walk in the spirit and stand before the foe, to the service and glory of God, by the strength received in the last two works of grace.[140]

The first work of grace is, most obviously, "justification and the new birth."[141] Our individual sinfulness and the Lord's work on the cross must first be inwardly and preveniently revealed to the unregenerate. Thereupon he has the opportunity either to reject the gospel or to experience repentance and the initial faith in Christ. In the latter he becomes a new creation and continues to live a life of maintained fellowship with God (process).

Much of what Nee says about this first step is neither new nor distinctive of his theology. Other Christians have written that in salvation the blood deals with a person's sins and is primarily for God, the cross is for the sinner and procures deliverance from the old man, and through Christ's substitutionary death the believer proceeds from death into eternal life.[142] But in Nee regeneration is also a phenomenon of the human spirit. In *The Spiritual Man* he writes:

> Man's spirit needs to be quickened because it is born dead. The new birth which the Lord spoke to Nicodemus is the new birth of the spirit. It certainly is not a physical birth as Nicodemus suspected, nor is it a soulical one. We must note carefully that the new birth imparts God's life to the *spirit* of man. Inasmuch as Christ has atoned for our soul and destroyed the principle of the flesh, so we who are joined to Him participate in His resurrecton life. We have been united with Him in His death; consequently it is in our spirit that we first reap the realization of His resurrection life. New birth is something which happens entirely within the spirit; it has no relation to soul or body.[143]

Again in *The Normal Christian Life* this premise serves as the structural base to his understanding of the Christian walk. While this teaching is not specifically stated here, Nee does quote Ezek. 36:26 as evidence that conversion is an act of the heart and of a new spirit, not a purification of the flesh.[144]

Likewise in both *The Spiritual Man* and *The Normal Christian Life* Nee envisions a conflict raging between a life according to the intuitive witness of the spirit and one according to the workings of the soul and the desires of the flesh.[145] Accordingly this conflict cannot be realized in the individual unless his spirit has been quickened/ made alive in conversion.

Deliverance from Sin

In the first work of grace man has become conscious that Jesus died for his sins upon the cross. In the second work of grace he becomes aware that he himself shares Christ's death. It is by grace that man is forgiven of his sins and is justified in God's sight, and it is also by God's grace that man is delivered from his own propensity to violate God's laws. It is this second work of grace that Nee calls "deliverance from sin."

Nee acknowledges that "this liberation from this power of sin . . . may be experienced the very hour a sinner accepts the Lord Jesus as Savior and is born anew."[146] Yet many more undergo a time of despair in their attempt to live a life worthy of God's calling. When one appropriates the blood of Christ that has dealt with *our sins,* Nee teaches, a civil war ensues in our hearts. For now our spirits daily strive against the life of the soul and its sin principle.

In the cross of Christ the sin principle is dealt with. Like justification and the new birth, deliverance from sin begins when a man realizes his utter sinfulness. He must see that justification has not eradicated the sin principle. In prayer, at the foot of the cross, the believer learns an important lesson in the Christian life: "knowing this, that our old man was crucified with Him, that the body of sin might be done away, so that we should no longer be in bondage to sin."[147] By the revelation of God's word we "know" that the crucifixion of the old man is an accomplished fact in God's eyes.

Experientially the believer responds in the crisis of his crucifixion and in the process of his resurrection. Paul exhorts the believer, "Reckon ye also yourselves to be dead unto sin, but alive unto God."[148] First the believer's old man, that is, his flesh, must be crucified. In this relinquishing of the life of the old man to the work of the cross, sin itself will no longer have dominion over the body.

Nowhere, Nee cautions, does the Scripture say that the root of sin within is eradicated, nor does God require man to suppress the body without (asceticism).[149] Until the glorification of our bodies the Christian can only sustain a life delivered from sin through the process of continual consecration.[150]

Nee's key texts for understanding consecration are Rom. 6:13, 16, 19 and 12:1-3.[151] On the basis of these texts Nee sees consecration as first an activity of the will, the third element of the soul, seeking to abide in Him.[152] Secondly, consecration involves a co-resurrection with

Christ, whereby the source of the Christian's life is God himself.[153] And thirdly, consecration's aim is to wait on God to serve Him.[154] Once the will has been so consecrated, the believer is "fully occupied with the divinity as well as the humanity of the Lord, with the divine strength and the unleavened life of the Lord, with the Holy Spirit and with the Lord's sensitivity."[155]

Prior to the believer's deliverance, the body sinned as a consequence of the old man. Once delivered the old man is reckoned as crucified, to the end that sin no longer has dominion over the body.

The first two works of grace have thus far quickened our spirits in salvation and freed our bodies from the power of sin. As yet the soul's nature has been unaffected.

Much of what these first two works of grace have done is remedial—undoing the damage done in man's fall in the Garden of Eden. The final two works are not remedial but are positive, in the direction of serving God's eternal purposes.[156] According to Nee, these purposes can best be comprehended through an analysis of God's commands in the Garden of Eden.[157] God commanded Adam to eat every tree except the tree of the knowledge of good and evil. The problem with this tree is that while man would no longer be ethically ignorant, he would also no longer be dependent upon God for his moral choice.

God did desire that he should partake freely of the fruit of the tree of life. And how does Nee perceive the meaning of this tree of life? It is God himself.

> . . . for God is life. He is the highest form of life, and He is also the source and goal of life. And the fruit: what is that? It is our Lord Jesus Christ. You cannot eat the tree

but you can eat the fruit. No one is able to receive God as God, but we can receive the Lord Jesus.[158]

Grace is therefore given so that the believer may more and more freely partake of the life-giving tree.

The Gift of the Holy Spirit

Much controversy has arisen in the contemporary church concerning the reception and evidence of the Pentecostal experience described in the second chapter of the Book of Acts. The same was true in China during the period of Watchman Nee's active ministry.[159] His own position is unlike that of traditional Pentecostal or modern charismatic theology.[160] Nee believes that the Spirit comes not through tarrying but through revelation. And that revelation is of Christ exalted upon His throne.[161] Thus the key text for realizing the Spirit outpoured is not Acts 1:4 but Peter's statement in 2:33-36. Once this is acknowledged by faith, then the crisis experience comes as the "Spirit outpoured."

The nature of the crisis experience, Nee emphasizes, is quite diverse. Citing the experiences of R.A. Torrey, Dwight L. Moody and Charles E. Finney,[162] Nee concludes that "we must leave God free to work as he wills" and "that each one whom the Spirit of God falls [sic] will unfailingly know it."[163]

The continued process is the Spirit indwelling, which is the very person of Jesus living in us. The Holy Spirit then provides us with the potential power to live the victorious life. But since it is Christ in us, that victory is only ours if we have "reverence" for Him and consciously recognize His presence.[164]

This idea of reverence for the exalted Christ permits Nee to speak of all Christians as having the Holy Spirit but not all having the Spirit outpoured/indwelling experience. This gift of the Holy Spirit experienced in a later working of the cross is one requiring a revelation of the fact of that indwelling at conversion. It is only then that the Spirit can begin to revolutionize the life of the believer.[165]

At this point in the believer's life, the Spirit indwelling within the human spirit is more and more making His presence felt in the human soul. But in order that the body may completely manifest the Spirit's bidding and be pleasing to God, the Christian must again receive further revelation from God.

Pleasing God

The fourth and final aspect of grace in the life of the believer is the most extensively written phase in Nee's writings. About half of *The Normal Christian Life* deals with this issue, and a majority of Nee's writings deal in some way with the practical aspect of "pleasing God."

Nee begins his discussion with an analysis of the meaning and value of Romans 7.[166] How does the Christian respond to the Old Testament law? The law is scriptural, and yet by trying to obey the law we are in essence denying the all-sufficiency of Christ. Nee understands the key to understanding Romans 7 is Rom. 7:18-19:

> For I know that in me, that is, in my flesh, dwelleth no good thing: for to will is present with me, but to do that which is good is not. For the good which I would I do not: but the evil which I would not, that I practice.[167]

In these verses is a summary of the purpose of the law and an important insight into the nature of the believer's service to God. The law sets for us a standard of what is good. But as Paul has stated in verse 19, the good is unattainable. For the law was written to show us that we cannot serve or do something for God. Using Paul's analogy in 7:1-4, only death can separate us from the law with its impossible requirements. Only then can we be united with Christ, the new husband, "who with every demand He makes becomes in . . . [us] the power for its fulfillment."[168] In order for us to fulfill the law we must put to death "the flesh," our "will" and our "doing." The revelation therefore for "pleasing God" is not an effort at trying to succeed in some established ethics or missionary goals but God's requirement for us to "cease from doing" through seeing the work of the cross. We are to stop trying to do God's will through our own will power, because such efforts are "soulical." For the only work of the church is one of justification and sanctification "through Jesus Christ our Lord" (7:25).

The continuing process of "pleasing God," to walk according to the Spirit (Rom. 8:4), is a task that constantly engages the faith of the spiritual man. His life is one of more and more of the Spirit enhancing, educating and refining himself by daily bearing the cross upon the soul life, to the end that he can declare with Paul that it is "no longer I but Christ in me."[169]

"The finished work of the cross," Nee writes, "and its continual application by the Holy Spirit are consequently inseparable."[170] Within Nee's trichotomy the Holy Spirit dwells within the human spirit. But in order for there to be a release of the Spirit, the soul must yield to the cross, just as the flesh yielded in justification. Our feelings must be crucified, for they by themselves will hinder God's work.[171] Our mind must be renewed through the work of the cross.[172] The will must also actively surrender itself at the foot of the cross to be preserved from Satan's lies.[173] The cross even brings victory over the power of physical death.[174]

In *The Release of the Spirit,* Nee succinctly presents the meaning of the work of the cross upon the soul and its affect upon our spirit:

> When we really understand the cross we shall see it means the breaking of the outward man viz., [the soul]. The cross reduces the outward man to death; it splits open the human shell. The cross must destroy all that belongs to our outward man—our opinions, our ways, our cleverness, our self-love, our all. The way is clear, in fact, crystal clear.
>
> As soon as our outward man is destroyed, our spirit can easily come forth.[175]

When the spirit, the agent and vehicle of the Holy Spirit in the church, is in a state of constant release as the cross works upon the soul, the body will do the work of God, and the believer will be as a spiritual man.

In understanding this principle it is possible to understand the extensive and meticulous attention that Nee's writings give on such matters as Bible study,[176] preaching,[177] prayer,[178] sleeping,[179] marriage,[180] family life,[181] witnessing,[182] separation from the world,[183] finance,[184] clothing and eating[185] and the church's life itself[186] through a highly allegorical method of exegesis. While a majority of Christian authors present certain biblical guidelines on such matters, Nee is concerned to present them in the light of his perception of what is "soulical" and what is spiritual. For the "soulical" man labors in vain, but the spiritual builds upon Christ, the true foundation.

5

The Church and Its Work

Historical Considerations

As we stated in chapter three of this book, conversion begins with the basic revelation of the gospel.* In most instances this revelation is transmitted through the proclamation of the word by members of a local church. Nee taught that the mere recitation of doctrine is not enough, however; for the word is also spiritual and must be communicated by spiritual men.† Thus whenever the church no longer had spiritual descendants committed to a personal faith in Christ, it was because the church had not produced men of the spirit.

Nee applauded the efforts of missionaries in China for producing many converts, but Nee faulted them for not producing men of the spirit, enabled by the grace of God to continue church growth independent of foreign missionaries.[1] Nee's solution was to produce a new church intent upon producing spiritual men and therefore a church of the Spirit.

Nee's concept of the church is perhaps the most controversial portion of his overall theology. Many who have wholeheartedly accepted his ideas on Bible study and his

---

*See p. 67-68.
†See p. 70-71.

concept of spirit/soul/body relationships have been reluctant to accept various aspects of his teachings on the church.

One book has already been written on the subject of Nee's church, James Mo-Oi Cheung's *The Ecclesiology of Watchman Nee and Witness Lee.* The book, originally written as a Master's thesis at Trinity Evangelical Divinity School, was suspended from sales shortly after its publication in 1972. As A. Donald Fredlund's letter states,* Mr. Cheung had made a serious error by consciously or unconsciously assigning Watchman Nee's *The Glorious Church* to Witness Lee. Despite this mistake Mr. Cheung has demonstrated that much of the Nee/Lee ecclesiology is derived from Plymouth Brethren theology and shares its tendency towards ecclesiastical exclusiveness.

Both Nee and Lee take care in distinguishing themselves from the Brethren in the matter of the ground of the local church. According to Nee's own testimony between 1921 and 1932, "What the Lord revealed to me was extremely clear: before long He would raise local churches in various parts of China. Whenever I closed my eyes, the vision of the birth of local churches appeared before my inward eyes."[2] What Nee is saying here and what is most explicit throughout his ecclesiastical works is that the local church of God cannot be further defined through adjectives such as Pentecostal, Nazarene, Episcopal, Roman Catholic, Protestant or even "gathered" as the Brethren did. It is only defined by the term local: its locality. Yet the basis of this teaching is very much an

____

*See Appendix A.

adjunct if not a theological expansion of the Brethren teaching on "the one assembly of God." C.H. Mackintosh, one of the greatest writers in Brethren theology, in his book *The Assembly of God* writes:

> We must now very briefly glance at what is the power by which the assembly is gathered. Here, again, man and his doings are set aside. It is not man's will, choosing; nor man's reason, discovering; nor man's judgment, dictating; nor man's conscience, demanding; it is the Holy Ghost gathering souls to Jesus. As Jesus is the only center, so the Holy Ghost is the only gathering power. The one is as independent of man as the other. It is "where two or three are *gathered*" [*sic*]. It does not say "where two or three are *met*." Persons may meet together round any centre, on any ground, by any influence, and merely form a club, a society, an association, a community. But the Holy Ghost gathers souls to Jesus on the ground of salvation; and this, wherever convened, is the principle of the Assembly of God, and nothing else is. It may consist of but "two or three," and there may be hundreds of Christians in the various religious systems around; yet would the "two or three" be on the ground of the Assembly of God.[3]

Nee was quite familiar with C.H. Mackintosh's writings, and he in fact presents arguments for an assembly ecclesiology in his *Assembly Together*.[4] Regardless of this Brethren "truth," Nee believed that to establish this doctrine as the basis of church fellowship was just as carnal as those established on the abilities of spiritual leaders or racial, material or social distinction within a local area.[5] Rather when God gathered His people in the New Testament it was always on the basis of the location named: Corinth, Ephesus, Rome, etc. And since every believer has the same Spirit of Christ within himself, every Christian must demonstrate the unity of that Spirit by attending one body in one locality. Latent within this view, though not explicitly expressed by Nee, is a dividing between those who listen to the unifying Spirit and join the local church movement and those who do not join the movement and are therefore not in tune with the Spirit's leading—between spiritual men and carnal men.*

Such a strong stand cannot be explained entirely by theological and exegetical considerations. Like many Chinese leaders[7] Nee was intolerant towards the inter-denominational rivalries and embarrassed by the disparity between the church's faith in the unity of the body of Christ and its own defense of sectarianism. Some in China endeavored to produce an "ecumenical spiritual unity" among the differing denominations by fellowshipping "spiritually."† Keeping within their sectarian status, these Christians would "stretch out their hands over the fence to hold hands on the other side." Nee rebuffed those offering such a solution:

> We cannot on the one hand covet fellowship and yet on the other hand have fellowship over fences. If we really desire fellowship, we must break down the fences and have fellowship. If we want to serve God and feel that all God's children should have fellowship, we must tear down all the fences to have fellowship. If the fences are right, then we must build the fences, not only ten feet high, but

---

*One of his successors, Witness Lee, is more explicit.[6]

†Most notably the China Inland Mission.[8]

ten thousand feet high. We must be thorough and absolute before God.[9]

For Nee the solution was to tear down the denominational fences and accept the spiritual and physical fellowship of his local churches—forming a single church denomination divided only on the basis of locality, as the churches are denominated in the New Testament.

As a gifted national leader in the Chinese church, Nee had the choice of either staying within the existing denominations or becoming an independent church. Either way the opportunity was there for Nee to choose his own ecclesiology, as well as the ecclesiology of his fellow workers and the flocks under his tutorial care.

His radical "Brethren" approach was most certainly motivated by one historical consideration: his thorough education in the spiritual piety of the Keswick and Brethren movements. From Brethren writers came the administrative outline of *The Normal Christian Church Life*; from Keswick speakers he identified the life of the church within the life of Christ emanating not from the carnal believer but from the spiritual man.

The Church Universal

Watchman Nee's concept of the church universal is very much a product of his central focus on the cross and its work upon the trichotomous man. "If we know the cross," Nee wrote, "in the way in which God means it to be known, we shall eventually find oneself within the Body [the Church]."[10] Since the first knowledge we receive about the cross—that Christ died for our sins—comes at conversion, Nee agreed with the Brethren theology that the minimum requirement for church fellowship and membership in the church is salvation, the presence of Christ's Spirit in man. The mere mental assent of man's soul was not enough. Membership comes as a result of revelation intuitively received by our quickened spirits.[11]

Conversion and membership in the church are also synonymous, because the church is Christ. Beyond that the nature and life of the church is to bring the exalted Christ unto the entire man. The church therefore is simultaneously fully Christ in its state and not fully Christ in its status. Nee explains the seemingly contradictory statement by seeing in the Bible two "Christs." The personal Christ is exalted upon the throne and has already won the victory. The corporate Christ, which is the personal Christ and the church, has not yet experienced the final victory. Only by the edification of the church through the proclamation of God's word and its resurrection in the *eschaton* can the church experience the full status of the personal exalted Christ.[12]

This close synonymity of Christ with the church is also present in Nee's discussion of the "Eve" typology of Eph. 5:22-32.[13] Since the church is Eve, he contends:

> The Church is composed only of that which is out of Christ. All man's talent, ability, thought, self and all that he has are outside the Church. Everything which comes from the natural man is outside the Church. Only that which comes out of Christ is in the Church. Eve was not made from clay, but from Adam, the one who typified Christ. The preciousness is that God took a rib from Adam and made Eve. Only that which came from Adam, not from clay, can be called "Eve," and only that which comes

out from Christ can be called the Church. All that is not from Christ has nothing to do with the Church.[14]

As a corollary to his assertion that the fleshly labors of carnal Christians are not a part of the church, the church universal is understood as originating from the sinless flesh of Christ and is therefore entirely sinless.

The Church Local

Perhaps the greatest weakness or failing in Watchman Nee's theology is in the practical expression of Christ's kingdom in the local church. While the underlying policies toward the church universal remained constant, his techniques of the church local underwent a serious change, in some instances a volte-face from his earlier prewar teachings. This ecclesiological change has also created a division within the present-day local church movement and generally a division between churches who favor the doctrines present in *The Normal Christian Church Life, What Shall This Man Do?* and *The Glorious Church* and those who adhere to the teachings present in *The Orthodoxy of the Church, Spiritual Authority* and *Further Talks on the Church Life.*

Nee's vision of the local church life style in the three earlier writings is most assuredly motivated by two concerns: a reexamination of the witness of Scripture and a theological interpretation of church history. What comes forth is the image of the church whose life is generated by the Holy Spirit in the life of man and is independent of any carnal ideologies.

The local church is local because the New Testament offers no other basis for division, according to Nee. Because it includes every Christian in a given restricted, geographical area* and because it has no authority over other churches, Nee feels, the church is safeguarded against a sectarian spirit. ". . . there is no scope for an able and ambitious false prophet to display his organizing genius by forming the different companies of believers into one fast federation and then satisfy his ambition by constituting himself as its head."[16] Theological heresies† are also in a sense quarantined to one church by reason of the church's isolationist polity.

In the defining of church offices Nee is also careful that each ministry be compartmentalized in a way that presumedly will not interfere in the spiritual life of the church. The first office defined in *The Normal Christian Church Life* is that of the apostle or, as perceived in the contemporary age, the missionary. As a Christian involved in the extralocal activity of the gospel, the missionary's authoritative sphere is uniquely governed by what Nee describes as the "Antioch" model of church growth. In Acts 13, Paul and Barnabas were commissioned by the Holy Spirit to establish other local churches. As apostles they could not rule at Antioch, for they were appointed to an extralocal ministry. Likewise they could not be elders in the churches they founded; but they could appoint elders in the new congregations. In this Nee believed that the Holy Spirit had established a ministry model that preserved the local character of the church—even the

---

*Nee defines local as a town or, in the case of a large city, a borough.[15]

†These include divisions on the basis of spiritual superheroes, the instrument of salvation, antisectarianism, doctrinal differences, racial, national and social differences.[17]

newly formed churches.

Within the church local it is the elders/bishops, appointed by the Holy Spirit in due season, who rule over the congregation. The two primary qualifications for an elder are that he be a member of the church there and that he be spiritually mature. This necessitates the Spirit's work in the congregation and in the apostles; personal preference must not interfere in the selection. Once appointed the elders rule and manage the work of the congregation. They can even refuse an apostle's entry into the assembly hall.[18]

In the governing policies of the local church Nee makes every effort to ensure that all things be done by the Spirit of God and not by any carnal motives. For example, businesses, hospitals, schools, charitable institutions and even Christian ministries must not be a part of the church. While these jobs can and should be done by spiritual men, they cannot detract from the real responsibilities of the church, being "the conducting of meetings for breaking of bread, for the exercise of spiritual gifts, for the study of the Word, for prayer, for fellowship and Gospel preaching."[19] No worker, whether he be an elder, an apostle or a holder of any office may receive a salary. He must live according to the free-will gifts received from Spirit-led brethren.

Underlying Nee's principle of church government is a strong reluctance to accept any form of organization. Instead the church must be an organism, dependent on the Spirit for its life. Even such faith missions as the China Inland Mission Nee suspected of having workers not entirely dependent on faith. For if one member lives by his faith in such "faith" missions, he must equally share what God has provided to the less faithful in the corporate mission structure. In summary, what emerges in these earlier writings is a decentralized, highly evangelistic movement originating out of Nee's concern for a rigid biblicism and that, "Everything which comes from the natural man is outside the church."[20]

However, the managerial policies avowed as biblical in *The Orthodoxy of the Church, Spiritual Authority* and *Further Talks on the Church Life* entirely differ from Nee's earlier writings and are reflective of differing historical circumstances. The church is no longer seeking to establish itself as a new theological front in a pagan society. Rather it is now an established church attempting to recover from the church's instability during the Japanese occupation, from the tempering of Nee's teaching authority as a result of his business entanglements at his brother's chemical firm and from the growing influence of Witness Lee. While these three books bear the imprimatur of Nee's name as author and his homiletical style, the organizational activism of Witness Lee is strongly present. It is Lee, described by Kinnear as "energetic and authoritarian, thriving on large numbers, and has a flair for organizing people,"[21] who is responsible for much of Nee's new ecclesiology that runs counter to Nee's earlier teachings. In the early local church it is the spiritual man, revealed out of Nee's own sufferings and Bible studies, who rules the congregation. But in the postwar era it is the spiritual man according to Witness Lee's authoritarian personality that takes charge in the local church.

In *The Orthodoxy of the Church,* the second and third chapters of Revelation are interpreted in a way that is critical of all other churches except the "local church." Written at a time when he was excommunicated from the Shanghai Church and Lee was his most faithful co-worker, Nee castigates Roman Catholics as the church of Thyatira, Protestants as Sardis and many of the Brethren as Laodicea. Nee's arguments are based on interpreting church history as a progressive recovery of the original truths of the Ephesus and Smyrna churches. While Nee always regarded other denominations with disfavor,* Nee here brings eschatological judgment upon all other churches:

> The Lord Jesus is the priest who walks in the midst of the churches to see which lamp is lighted and which one is not. The trimming is the judgement, for the judgement begins in the house of God. Christ walks in the midst of the churches doing the work of judgement, and today's judgement is seen from eternity.[23]

> All those who study the Bible know that the problem of choosing the Roman Catholic Church is over. The difficulty lies here: that is, many brothers do not know that the problem of choosing the Protestant churches is also over. Does the Lord want us to be in Sardis? Strangely enough, many are rather satisfied to be in Sardis. But as we read the Word of God, the Lord will show us that He is not satisfied with Sardis. The Lord's desire is Philadelphia.[24]

According to Nee's book only some Brethren and the local church are the faithful overcomers who are the

---

*Nee's antidenominationalism created problems among co-workers as early as 1923.[22]

church of Philadelphia. Here the words of Nee are "spiritual" in sound as are his earlier writings, but a bitter note rings now.

In chapter six of *Further Talks on the Church Life*, the doctrine of Jerusalem principle is presented. According to this "light" of God's truth the work of the church is regional, and therefore the work must proceed, not from every local church, but from a regional center.[25] According to this plan workers from the differing congregations go to one of these regional centers and are trained for two months to one year. From there they either return to their own local churches as leaders or go off to one of the unchurched mission fields. Out of experiences learned during the war years, missionaries are now sent out or "migrated" in groups of twenty to forty.[26]

In this same chapter, while offering his continuing support of the revelation of "locality," Nee nullifies the practical reality of the local churches' independence. Nee tells his trainees, "Therefore, brothers, when you, a co-worker, reside in a locality, you are there as both an apostle and an elder."[27] Thus the regional center governs all other local churches, not through an episcopal control, as is the case in Roman Catholic, Episcopal and Methodist churches, but through a pedagogic control.

The dynamics of this polity work on the principle that there are spiritual men capable of teaching others to do the "work." As practiced in the postwar local church in China there are actually only two "spiritual men" who are doing the teaching: Watchman Nee and Witness Lee. Whether a co-worker trained in the regional center at Shanghai or Foochow, the training lessons were the same—standardized by Nee's and Lee's revelations on the meaning of God's word. Then a group of these newly trained co-workers would be sent into the local church to increase the church's membership and aid the old members with their spiritual teachings. Invariably they did increase the membership more rapidly than the less organized methods of the independent local church. By their successful efforts and with the support of the new members, these trained co-workers became the new elders of the expanding local church, and they are able to override the decisions of the older elders. While the Nee/Lee takeover usually went smoothly, the local church in Foochow split in two in 1948, and through Witness Lee's efforts the Hong Kong local church became bitterly divided over the admission of co-workers as elders in 1970.[28]

Added to this was a new dimension to the importance of the spiritual man in the local church movement. Prior to this period, it was understood that all the differing works of grace were open to all and everyone was capable of reaching the highest earthly plateau of Christian maturity. But in the new local church a spiritual hierarchy was unconsciously being established with Watchman Nee first, then Witness Lee, then the workers/elders taught at one of the training centers, then the rest of the men and finally the women, who must wear veils out of submission.[29] Kinnear even reports that a row of chairs were set up in each meeting place for the top echelon, in which the number one seat was unanimously reserved for Nee.[30] The theological-spiritual basis for this development was given to co-workers during their training and is preserved in the book *Spiritual Authority*.

In *Spiritual Authority,* Nee argues that to disobey the authorities delegated by God in the church (e.g., elders) and in the world is to disobey and be in rebellion against God:

> People will perhaps argue, "What if the authority is wrong?" The answer is, If God dares to entrust His authority to men, then we can dare to obey. Whether the one in authority is right or wrong does not concern us, since he has to be responsible directly to God. The obedient needs only to obey; the Lord will not hold us responsible for any mistaken obedience, rather will He hold the delegated authority responsible for his erroneous act. Insubordination, however, is rebellion, and for this the one under authority must answer to God.[31]

Nee also enumerates the characteristics that he expects to be found in God's delegated authorities. A total of five pages is devoted to the ethical requirements of eldership; a total of seventy pages is devoted to the spiritual qualifications.

The Church in the Eschaton

Much of what Nee presents in his biblical anthropological texts tends toward a kind of bifurcation between the spiritual and carnal Christian. In the eschatology of *Come, Lord Jesus, God's Plan and the Overcomers* and *Love Not the World* the final destination of the church is also divided between the saved and the "overcomers":

> Only the overcoming believers are related to the new city during the millennial kingdom. In the new heaven and new earth, both the saved and the overcomers partake equally in New Jerusalem.

The wedding gown is worn only for a time; the believers who overcome are joined together as the bride.

At the marriage of the Lamb it looks as though the door
of the New Jerusalem is opened for the first time to let in
the overcomers. The foolish virgins are not able to enter
at this time.[32]

In support of this Nee identifies the 144,000 in Rev. 7:4-8
as the Jews who will rule with Christ; the 144,000 in 14:1
are the overcoming "virgins" who are representative of
the larger group of "overcomers" in the church. While
the former will reign with Christ among the nations during the millennium, the latter are caught up in the air and
simultaneously reign in the heavenlies.[33] While all Christians have a place in the new heaven and earth, only these
overcomers enter into the new Jerusalem during the 1,000
years.

Since the "overcomers" are a prominent part of the
seven letters of Revelation 2 and 3, Nee presupposes that
in the modern church only those who have experienced
the historic recovery of the Philadelphia church—the
spiritual Christians of the Brethren and local church
movements—will share in the heavenly millennial reign
of Christ.

In both *Love Not the World* and *God's Plan and the
Overcomers* Nee draws on the overcoming imagery of
Revelation to affirm victory over Satan, the prince of this
world. But the victory over Satan in the world "demands
an utterness of spirit Godward that in itself effectively
deprives Satan of any moral ground in us he may claim to
possess."[34] Because they are spiritually mature, not only
will the overcomers share Christ's kingdom in the coming

age, but they will also institute that reign by ascending to heaven in the rapture:

> When they are on earth, Satan has no retreat; and when they ascend to heaven, Satan is cast down. Victory lies in regaining the ground. The man child conquers on behalf of the mother [Rev. 12:5-10]: the overcomers win the victory for the church. Moreover, in the end time, God uses overcomers to conclude the war in heaven. These overcomers shall bring "the salvation, and the power, and the kingdom of our God, and the authority of his Christ" into heaven. The serpent therefore has no more place in heaven. Hence wherever the overcomers are, Satan is forced to retreat.[35]

The judicial division between the carnal saved and the spiritual overcomers is also applied to the believer's present resting place after death. Pressed by the need to make distinctions between believers, Nee is forced into accepting a Protestant form of purgatory. When questioned about the people in Heb. 6:4-6 in the book *Gospel Dialogue,* Nee interprets the context as dealing with Christian progress and not with a falling away from salvation. Accordingly, the people in Hebrews 6 are identified as Christians living in sin according to works who must be refined through a limited period of punishment.[36]

Admittedly the identification of the overcomers with Nee's spiritual men is not directly stated in any of his eschatological discourses. Nevertheless the identification is communicated by his use of the same idioms and expressions of his spiritual anthropology in his description of the overcomers. For example, since the work of the cross also divides overcomers from the rest of the saved,[37]

it is most certain that the carnal/spiritual division of
believers is synonymous or parallel to his eschatological
dichotomy of overcomers and other Christians. Historically this is again in evidence in the close tie with
Nee's spiritual life/man teachings and his partial rapture
theory. M.E. Barber, who tutored Nee in the Keswick
approach to spiritual dynamics, assuredly taught him a
partial rapture theory. For the theory originated in the
writings of Robert Govett (1813-1901), who, after leaving
the Anglican Church, founded Surry Chapel, Norwich. As
was stated in chapter one, Miss Barber was sent out from
this same chapel as an independent missionary. Nee even
admits in his lecture on the Book of Revelation, published
as *Come, Lord Jesus,* his dependence on Govett's *The
Apocalypse Expounded* (1920)[38]—no doubt borrowed
from Miss Barber's library.

6

Summary and Conclusions

The first chapter of this book presented a number of historical details quite significant in understanding and appreciating Nee's theology. Raised in a cultural setting that was both Oriental and an admixture of Occidental practice and Christian proclamation, Nee's conversion and early ministry were marked by his own struggle of conscience between biblical demand and human practice. First, Nee despaired over his inability to serve the Lord in conformance to the witness of Scripture and the convictions of his conscience. Secondly, his mind was preoccupied with finding some way of purifying the evangelical witness in China of any purely Western, nonbiblical elements. The first conflict Nee resolved during a lengthy illness by discriminating between "carnal" and "spiritual" believers on the basis of their appropriation of the work of the cross of Christ. The second goal resulted in his establishment of a new indigenous church based on the principle of "locality" and "spiritual" leadership. While he changed some of his views on the church, both Nee and his successors continued to distinguish between the "carnal" and the "spiritual" side of Christian faith.

In chapter two the style and content of his literature were examined for evidence of continuity. Whether it be in the early years of his career or in the last years before

143

his imprisonment, all of his material was written or spoken in a devotional, expository form that emphasized the "spiritual reality" of the Bible and the "normal Christian life."

The succeeding three chapters offered an analysis of Nee's fundamental teachings. Like Karl Barth, Nee is deeply concerned with the word of God both as Scripture and as church proclamation. On the basis of his belief in God's perfecting grace in the life of the spiritually minded, he concludes that the interpretation and preaching of Scripture can be inerrant in its communication of spiritual life. Far more elaborate and complex than his writings on the Word, his teachings on anthropology are also based on a trichotomous division of man into spirit, soul and body. Without these elements being in proper relationship with one another and with God, Nee contends, the normal Christian life is impossible. Likewise the church's life cannot be normal unless it is structured in a way that produces spiritual men and excludes the heresy and divisions brought about by the "soulish" or carnal believer. In fact, the ultimate destination of the church is divided between those who are merely saved and those who are "spiritual."

On the basis of historical and literary research, therefore, certain conclusions can be drawn concerning the nature and significance of Watchman Nee as a church leader and expositor:

1. The growing need for reform in the church of China serves as the historical *Sitz im Leben* ("life situation") for Nee's beliefs. The indigenous movement within the church and antimissionary sentiments without are

important factors in understanding the radical content and direction of Nee's teachings.

2. The reform of the church through the spiritual reform of the Christian offered by Nee and the Local Church originated in Nee's tutelage in Keswick and Brethren theology.

3. Concern for the spiritual condition of the believer is a persistent theme throughout Nee's preaching career.

4. In Nee's theology Scripture can only be comprehended, communicated and perceived as the living word of God by means of an intrapsychic working of the Holy Spirit in the believer.

5. The Christian is a trichotomous being. By the Holy Spirit quickening a man's fallen spirit, the believer is a union of body, soul and spirit. Each element has its own functions and its own requirements for spiritual health.

6. The Christian life which Nee deems "normal" comes by the differential working of grace on the spirit, soul and body.

7. The church consists of both spiritual and carnal Christians.

8. The New Testament church is interpreted as having a structure that inhibited the works of the carnal believer (heresies, sectarianism, etc.) and encouraged the works of the spiritual believer. In Nee's thought that structure was governed either by the principle of "locality" or by the pedagogic authority of the spiritual man.

9. At Christ's return the spiritual Christians who have overcome the world will play a different part in the millennial reign than will the carnally minded believers. The spiritual man will reign with Christ in the heavenlies; the

carnal man will reign with Christ on earth among the nations.

In summary, driven by an intense desire to have more of Christ's life and power manifest in China, Nee's notion of the spiritual man became the determinate foundation that gave substance to his doctrine of revelation, Scripture, sanctification, perfection, ecclesiology and eschatology.

An Evangelical Assessment

To read any of the books ascribed to Watchman Nee is sure to create strong opinions as to the potential value of his ideas. During the past five years I have interviewed many pastors, teachers, seminary students and informed laymen in order to find some majority consensus. Some praised Nee for his insights into the nature of the Christian church and its spiritual life. A few described how churches have experienced renewal as a result of studying one or more of his books. Yet others upbraided Nee for false doctrine and unconsciously providing a convenient theology for such cult groups as The Way, The Children of God and The Alamo Foundation. A few described how spiritual pride, fostered by Nee's division of spiritual and carnal believers, had divided congregations.

The ambiguity of these responses gives some indication that a simple dismissal or unqualified support of Watchman Nee is inappropriate. Watchman Nee was unquestionably a witness imprisoned because of the word of God and the testimony he maintained. Yet as a writer within the broad spectrum of evangelicalism read largely by evangelicals, Nee's teaching and preaching legacy should be subject to the plumb line of God's Word, the

Bible. Upon this basis, certain of Nee's doctrines and presuppositions are certainly questionable.

Nee is admirable and insightful in understanding the illuminating work of divine revelation in comprehending the spiritual reality of the Bible. But he also seems unappreciative of the Bible as God's interpretation of real events, language, culture and people in His covenant history. In Nee's discussions of Bible study methods, comparing and compiling texts are his keys to understanding, never the historical circumstances of the passages. Like many writers who rely entirely on the devotional hermeneutic, he never subjects the biblical text to some discerning questions: Why does the author say this? How does it fit into the context of the whole book? Does the historical background of the passage relate to the circumstances of my own life or the life of my church?

Particularly in interpreting anthropological terms, Nee's method is far too often a lexical search through Young's or Cruden's concordance, where historical or literary context is not under consideration. In 1 Thess. 5:23, for example, is Paul making a statement about biblical anthropology or is he using the language of his opponents? The latter does more justice to the biblical evidence. Paul is writing to a church unable to fit physical death and physical labor into their theology. We know for certain that some forms of Greek gnostic philosophy during this period saw the spirit in opposition to the limitations of the soul and body.* If Paul is opposing the

---

*That gnosticism is at issue here is evident in that "soul" in a psychological sense appears only in Paul's letters to the Thessalonians and Corinthians where belief in a future, physical, resurrection was a problem.

syncretizing of this view with Christian faith, then 1 Thess. 5:23 is not saying that spirit, soul and body are entirely distinct human entities. Rather, Paul is saying that the ongoing sanctification in Christ until the second coming involves the whole man ("through and through").

Or Heb. 4:12. Is the dividing asunder by the word of God a distinguishing of two parts of man's nature (soul and spirit), as Nee contends? Or does the dividing of the word of God involve a judgment on whether the thoughts and attributes of the heart are from man (soul) or from God (Spirit)? The entire context of Hebrews 4 suggests that we are dealing with the motives of the heart, not with some intrapsychic battle of a human spirit with the soul.

This compilation of proof texts apart from the rigors of undertstanding context is certainly compatible to the "amens" of the spiritually enlightened. But there are dangers to such an understanding of Scripture. First, spiritual exegesis often leads to a "canon within the canon." Churches and movements that have entirely "sought" to touch the spiritual reality of the Bible through the prayer methods described in Nee's *The Ministry of God's Word* and *Ye Search the Scriptures* often neglect the narrative portions that deal with the humanness of God's revelation. There is no earthly life of Jesus discernible in the writings of Nee; rather it is the resurrected Christ of doctrinal theology that Nee continually homilizes. The historical books of the Old Testament are only touched upon whenever they use some anthropological terms or as they foreshadow the finished work of Christ. The prophets are discussed for their prediction of the redemptive future, not when they proclaim judgment upon the social injustices of their own age. While as a matter of evangelical faith Nee affirms the sixty-six books of the Bible, in practice his words have depicted the canon as a more spiritual, less historical book.

Secondly, Nee's ahistorical, spiritual understanding of the Bible infers that the church's spiritual life is unconcerned with the physical reality of war, famine and injustice. Like Jessie Penn-Lewis's magazine, *Overcomer,* Nee writes without reference to the inordinate suffering of the Chinese during World War II. While the social ethicists of modern liberalism ignore the spiritual dimension of God's kingdom, the pietism underlying Nee's view of Scripture has lost sight of the social concern of such passages as Amos 2:6-8, Luke 14:12-14 and James 5:1-5.

Finally Nee's spiritual exegesis, mixed with a shift toward a more monarchial form of government, led to the phenomena of Witness Lee and the Local Church. From the beginning Watchman Nee's preaching eloquence led many to honor and admire him to a degree beyond the range of critical judgment or the New Testament's demand to test the spirits of events and teachings within the congregation. Those like Leland Wang who disapproved were never permitted any congregational expression of grievances and inevitably left. Those who remained were more docile to the teachings of their elders and insensitive to the changes taking place in the church's doctrines and leadership.

Fundamentally the idea of spiritual exegesis is not foreign to New Testament Christianity. Every believer to a varying degree has a tremendous advantage over the secular man in comprehending the Bible because of his relationship in Christ. Yet such a method of prayer and meditation opted by the spiritual exegete is not without its dangers. When the Christian message of the resurrection had become too spiritualized in the Corinthian community, Paul provided correction in the recounting of the history of Christ's resurrection appearances (1 Cor. 15:3-9). Likewise, today, separated as we are by the cultural and historic changes of two millennia, both private and public proclamation must accord with the historic accounts and revelations given in the Bible within its cultural (Semitic and Hellenistic) setting.

Beyond the problem in biblical exegesis, Nee's discrimination between what is acceptably human, the spirit, and what is unacceptably human, the soul, in our spiritual life creates an introspective life. Christian faith is not perceived as a sacrificial offering of ourselves to God, a life "in Christ" and a community set apart from worldly values. Nee instead offers "laws of the spirit," definitions of soulical and spiritual, and mind analysis in order to receive full salvation.[1] While some of his works, like *The Normal Christian Life,* rightly have the cross as its bench mark, others, such as *The Latent Power of the Soul* and *The Spiritual Man,* teach us gnostic psychoanalysis. In the latter the key to Christian maturity is not something easily discernible to the born-again believer. Rather, by extensive Bible studies supplemented by the "spiritual knowledge" of the mature and a series of spiritual enlightenments, one can receive full salvation.

True spirituality, however, is an activity of the Holy

Spirit and is therefore God's gracious gift. It can not be fulminated by obeying a list of psychic commandments. The Holy Spirit as sanctifier admonishes us whenever we are living according to our own desires (the flesh) and encourages us when we live according to God's will (the Spirit). Whether one understands the characteristics of the soul and the "human spirit" is irrelevant. Once sin is made known, continuing growth is conditioned upon repentance and surrendering ourselves more to the work of the Holy Spirit.*

Nee's description of the "carnal man" and the "soulical man" can and does quite powerfully expose that part of the Christian personality that continues to function by its own strength quite independently of God's power. It may therefore be even true that some intrapsychic laws are in operation. But it is altogether unnecessary to be able to recite them to serve God more abundantly. Indeed, sanctification preconditioned upon our comprehension of the hidden mechanics of the spiritual man may lead to a spirit of pride rather than to a humble and contrite heart.

It is this pride of knowledge which also flaws the quality of Nee's idea on the church and its life. In particular Nee's rejection of any local church that does not denominate itself on the basis of a geographical locality is another example of his hidden wisdom from the Bible. Followers of Witness Lee and Watchman Nee who have banded together to form "local churches" believe that the "recovery" of this doctrine makes them more faithful to God's plan of the church. However, the Bible never commands us to

---

*Rom. 12:1.

label our churches in a particular way. The Bible does command and commend the fruits or works of righteousness by the power of Christ's Spirit within us.

Finally we must fault Nee in his teachings on pastoral authority, a fault that has been the most destructive to the evangelical witness of Christ in the contemporary church. According to the Scriptures the church's mission is to proclaim the King of kings and His kingdom, but Nee seems to have made God's lieutenants, the elders, local monarchs themselves. The local church elders described in *Spiritual Authority* have unquestioned authority. Such authoritativeness is inappropriate to God's elect, who proclaim God's sovereign rule in their lives. The Epistle to the Hebrews does say, "Obey them that have rule over you" (13:7). But to the author of Hebrews obeying an elder is following his example by proclaiming the Word of God to others, emulating his Christian life and imitating his faith in God (13:7). As the word "elder" implies, leaders arise in the church not by their dominating personality, nor by their preaching ability, but by the maturity of their relationship with Christ as Lord of their lives.*

Nee's whole spiritual philosophy assumes that the mature who give direction are elected by God for their spiritual "charisma." A tranquil face, a peaceful smile and a spiritual aura that condescends to the "unspiritual" become the trademarks of the leader in such superspiritual churches. In contrast, Christ set an example for us, in the washing of the disciples' feet, of a leader who is a servant not a spiritual prince. While Nee's version of a charis-

---

*The shepherds of God's flock feed Christ's sheep, not rule them (John 21:16).

matic leader appeals to the contemporary culture's quest and infatuation with the gnostic guru, it is not Christlike. What the church needs today are leaders who demonstrate to us the fruit of righteousness in the manner of one of God's faithful servants.

Nee himself became for some Christian readers a spiritual guru, a mystic intermediary between Christ and the struggling believer. For them he "recovered" the key to becoming spiritual. His style and message became a guide in determining the value of other Christian writers. Those that lacked the spiritual flavor of Nee's words were dismissed as carnal or tainted by the power of the soul.

But many more Christians read with a discerning eye. They did not enjoy or agree with every book ascribed to Watchman Nee. They read books by Christians of different literary styles and temperaments. Yet Nee taught many of us a greater appreciation of how Christ's death on the cross has given us the victory. For this alone the name of Watchman Nee is worthy of double honor (1 Tim. 5:17).

Appendix A.

Apology of A. Donald Fredlund and James Mo-Oi Cheung
April 19,1973

TO WHOM IT MAY CONCERN:

Following publication of the book THE ECCLESIOLOGY OF WATCHMAN NEE AND WITNESS LEE by James Mo-Oi Cheung, we received personal visits and letters from associates of Witness Lee who asserted that he does not hold or teach some of the views that were attributed to him in the book. Accordingly, C.L.C. [Christian Literature Crusade] as publisher has taken the following actions:

1) Eight days after the book was first offered for sale, we removed the appendix in toto and rebound the remaining stock because of material in the appendix that we could not substantiate in light of the new information.
2) In mid-February we stopped all further sale of the book when it was brought to our attention that material which we could not substantiate was present in the body of the book as well.
3) We wrote a letter of apology to Mr. Witness Lee regarding imputations of heresy, etc., that the book contained.

4) We suspended publication of a revised and corrected edition of the book.
5) We issued a recall, for full credit, of all copies of the book sold.
6) We agreed that C.L.C. would not publish a revised edition of the book.

We feel that we owe to all parties interested in this publication a fuller explanation of the reasons for the actions detailed above. The following statement is intended to be the vehicle by which the author and publisher acknowledge that items in the areas mentioned below should not, for lack of supporting evidence, have appeared in the book. At the same time we do not mean to suggest that all believers would agree to all the teachings of Witness Lee and his associates.

Assertions by associates of Witness Lee that the book misrepresents him with respect to doctrine fall in these general areas:

1) Imputations of heresy to Witness Lee specifically in reference to his views on the blood of Jesus and the person and nature of Jesus Christ.
2) The claim that in matters of doctrine Witness Lee differs substantially from the views held by Watchman Nee (differences are evidently much narrower than suggested by the book).
3) The inference that Witness Lee resorts to deliberate "twisting of Scripture" or "misuse of the Word."
4) The allegation that Witness Lee holds to a strict "baptismal regeneration" view of baptism.

In addition, the authorship of the book THE GLORIOUS CHURCH was incorrectly attributed to Witness Lee, whereas the author was in fact Watchman Nee. We want it to be known that it is not our policy to disseminate material concerning any person or persons that is known to be inaccurate.

We sincerely regret feelings of offense created by the publication of this book, as well as any inconvenience caused by its subsequent recall and termination.

Sincerely in Christ,
CHRISTIAN LITERATURE CRUSADE

A. Donald Fredlund   James Mo-Oi Cheung
Publications Secretary   Author

Appendix B.

On The Spiritual Man. *Fourth Editorial of Revival Magazine,
April 3, 1952*

[The following editorial is recorded in C.T. Chan's *My
Uncle Watchman Nee,* pp. 118-120. It appears here for
the first time in English, translated by Miss Joyce Leung
and Mr. Wing-Tai Leung.]

The revised edition of *The Spiritual Man* has been sent
to the publisher. The book was received very well. Those
who just read the book, but have not received God as
Savior, are going against the truth of the book.

During the past two years, there has been a revival in
the church everywhere. That's God's power at work. But
partly that is nature, supernature, at work too, not totally
spiritual. The aim of *The Spiritual Man* is to point out the
two themes to make people understand what is bad
naturally; what is bad supernaturally; what is spiritual;
and what is a bad influence. Those who have accepted
Christ and the cross will have no problem distinguishing
them.

Dramatic work and spiritual work can't be mixed. The
flesh enjoys dramatic work, because it stimulates one's
emotions. So when one first sees truth he accepts it, but
that doesn't mean that the truth is his. He has to pay for

it. Many times the payment is agony in feeling. And many fail because they can't do it.

I am not against supernatural things. The Bible records many precious strange miracles. And I am not against people seeking for miracles; in fact, I encourage people to do so. But I would like to distinguish between miracles and the spiritual life. The former is not as precious as the latter. Besides, supernatural miracles can come from God or from the Devil (false spiritual work). So I would like to find out their differences from the Bible so everybody can differentiate them.

A passive commission and an empty mind are very dangerous. I hope the readers of *The Spiritual Man* can really understand it and avoid these pitfalls.

Most people ask me about the dates of the revised edition. We cannot tell or fix it yet. Maybe after, we hope the brothers will be united in heart and spirit, lest there be errors.

The servant of the Family of Christ
Watchman Nee

© 1970 The China Alliance Press, from the book *My Uncle Watchman Nee* by Stephen C.T. Chan. Used by permission.

Notes

Introduction

1. Michael Harper, *As at the Beginning: The Twentieth Century Pentecostal Revival* (Plainfield, N.J.: Logos International, 1965), pp, 51-79; Walter J. Hollenweger, *The Pentecostals: The Charismatic Movement in the Churches* (Minneapolis: Augsburg Publishing House, 1972), pp. 3-17; John Thomas Nichol, *The Pentecostals* (Plainfield, N.J.: Logos International, 1966), pp. 240-45; and John L. Sherrill, *They Speak with Other Tongues,* Spire ed. (Westwood N.J.: Fleming H. Revell Co., 1965), pp. 51-67.
2. For a history of the movement: Ronald M. Enroth, Edward E. Ericson, Jr., and C. Breckinridge Peters, *The Jesus People: Old Time Religion in the Age of Aquarius* (Grand Rapids: Wm. B. Eerdmans Publishing Co., 1972), pp. 21-157.
3. Rev. Edwin Stube to Dana Roberts, Feb. 16, 1975, personal letter.
4. Ellis Leif Larson, "Where Preachers Dare! (An Empirical Evaluation of the Church Renewal Phenomena in the 1960's)" (Ann Arbor, Mich.: University Microfilms, 73-10, 251, 1972).
5. Watchman Nee, *Ye Search the Scriptures* (New York: Christian Fellowship Publishers, Inc., 1974), p. 15.

Notes

Chapter 1

1. Marcel Girard, ed., *Nagel's Encyclopedia-Guide: China* (Geneva: Nagel Publications, 1968), p. 1157.
2. Edmund J. Wehrle, *Britain, China and the Antimissionary Riots, 1891-1900* (Minneapolis: University of Minnesota, 1966), p. ix.
3. Robert Philip, *Peace with China! or, The Crisis of Christianity in Central Asia: A Letter to the Right Honourable T.B. Macauly, Secretary at War.* (London: John Snow, 1840), p. 4.
4. Tang Tse-Shing, *Death Blow to Corrupt Doctrines: A Plain Statement of Facts* (Shanghai: The Gentry and People, 1870), p. 13.
5. Peter S. Goertz, "A History of the Chinese Indigenous Christian Church under the American Board in Fukien Province" (Ph.D. dissertation, Yale University, 1933), p. 165.
6. Rev. R. Anderson to S.F. Woodin, December 31, 1863, American Board of Missions, Foochow Missionaries Document Vol. 301, Harvard University, Cambridge, Mass. Angus Kinnear [*The Story of Watchman Nee: Against the Tide* (Fort Washington, Pa.: Christian Literature Crusade, 1973), p. 20.] is incorrect in saying that U-Cheng was the first to be ordained. Mission records show that Ding Long-Go was ordained on April 23, 1876, one month earlier than Nga U-Cheng. Anderson to Woodin, June 30, 1876.
7. Kinnear, *Against the Tide*, p. 23. The quote is not cited in his notes, but it is probably from Nee Lin Ho-P'ing, *En Ai Piao Pen* [An Object of Grace and Love] (Shanghai, 1943).
8. Juvenal 6. 602; Lactantius *The Divine Institutes* bk. 6. 20; Tertullian *Ad Nationes* 15.
9. W.S. Packenham-Walsh, *Twenty Years in China* (Cambridge: W. Heffer & Sons Ltd., 1935), p. 95.
10. Packenham-Walsh, *Twenty Years*, p. 5.
11. Watchman Nee, *Watchman Nee's Testimony*, comp. K.H. Weigh (Hong Kong: Church Book Room Ltd., 1974), pp. 11-12.
12. There is a disparity of accounts concerning the date of Miss Yu's revival meeting. In Leslie T. Lyall's *Three of China's Mighty Men* [(London: Overseas Missionary Fellowship, 1973), p. 52] the date is set at the end of 1919; in Kinnear's *Against the Tide* (pp. 32-33), at the end of February 1920; in *Watchman Nee's Testimony* (p. 10), April of the same year; and both C.T. Chan's *My Uncle Watchman Nee* [Wo-Ti Kau Fu Nee To-Sheng (Hong Kong: The Alliance Press, 1970), p. 7] and James Mo-Oi Cheung's *The Ecclesiology of Watchman Nee and Witness Lee* [(Fort Washington, Pa.:

Christian Literature Crusade, 1972), pp. 14-15] as late as 1922. Cheung and Chan have apparently confused the events of Nee's conversion with that of his "baptism in the Holy Spirit."

13. Kinnear, *Against the Tide,* p. 33.

14. Ibid., p. 34.

15. Nee, *Testimony,* p. 10.

16. Watchman Nee, *A Living Sacrifice,* Basic Lesson Series, vol. 1 [trans. Stephen Kaung] (New York: Christian Fellowship Publishers, Inc., 1972), p. 30.

17. Idem, *The Spiritual Man,* 3 vols. [trans. Stephen Kaung] (New York: Christian Fellowship Publishers, Inc., 1968), 1:88-89.

18. Idem, *Testimony,* p. 12.

19. Nee, *Testimony,* p. 15.

20. Ibid., p. 17-18.

21. Ibid., p. 25.

22. Ibid., p. 24.

23. Rom. 6:3; Mark 16:16; Nee, *The Good Confession,* Basic Lesson Series, vol. 2 [trans. Stephen Kaung] (New York: Christian Fellowship Publishers, Inc., 1973), pp. 21-22; idem, *Living Sacrifice,* p. 13.

24. Lyall, *Mighty Men,* p. 56.

25. Kinnear, *Against the Tide,* pp. 48, 78.

26. For a history of these two events see Steven Barabas, *So Great Salvation: The History of the Keswick Convention* (London: Marshall, Morgan & Scott, 1952); David Matthews, *I Saw the Welsh Revival* (Chicago, Moody Press, 1951); Rev. J. Vyrnwy Moran, *The Welsh Religious Revival 1904-5: A Retrospect and a Criticism* (London: Chapman & Hall Ltd., 1909); Jessie Penn-Lewis, *The Awakening in Wales* (Dorset, England: The Overcomer Literature Trust, n.d.); John Pollock, "A Hundred Years of Keswick," *Christianity Today,* June 20, 1975, pp. 6-8; and G. Campbell Morgan and W.T. Stead, *The Welsh Revival* (Boston: The Pilgrim Press, 1905).

27. Idem, *The Centrality of the Cross* (Dorset, England: The Overcomer Literature Trust, n.d.), pp. 7, 25.

28. Ibid., pp. 19, 23; idem, *The Cross of Calvary* (Dorset, England: The Overcomer Literature Trust, n.d.), pp. 35, 37-40, 62-63.

29. Kinnear, *Against the Tide,* p. 50.

30. Watchman Nee, *The Orthodoxy of the Church* (Los Angeles: The Stream Publishers, 1970), pp. 73-74.

31. 1 Cor. 11:26.

32. Watchman Nee, *Twelve Baskets Full,* 6 vols. (Hong Kong: Hong-Kong Church Book Room, 1966), 2:38-39.

33. Idem, *Spiritual Reality or Obsession* [trans. Stephen Kaung] (New York: Christian Fellowship Publishers, Inc., 1970), passim.

34. Kinnear, *Against the Tide,* p. 73.

35. Watchman Nee, *Orthodoxy,* pp. 86-96.

36. Ibid., p. 95.

37. Idem, *The Latent Power of the Soul* [trans. Stephen Kaung] (New York: Christian Fellowship Publishers, Inc., 1972), p. 49.

38. Witness Lee, *The Baptism in the Holy Spirit* (Los Angeles: The Stream Publishers, 1969), p. 12.

39. Nee, *Latent Power,* pp. 48-54; idem, *Spiritual Man,* 1:38-39, 169.

40. Interview with Mrs. Carol Stearns, Church at Hollis, Hollis, New York, October 14, 1972.

41. Kinnear, *Against the Tide,* p. 104.

42. Walter J. Hollenweger, "Unusual Methods of Evangelism in the Pentecostal Movement in China," *A Monthly Letter about Evangelism* nos. 8/9 (November/December 1965); Stanley H. Frodsham, *With Signs Following* (Springfield, Mo.: Gospel Publishing House, 1946), pp. 121-141.

43. Keswick Convention Trustees, *The Keswick Convention 1938* (London: Pickering & Inglis Ltd., 1938), p. 245.

44. Watchman Nee, *The Normal Christian Life* (Fort Washington, Penn.: Christian Literature Crusade, 1961), pp. 106-21. On this chapter one scholar has said: "L' exégèse du chapitre'de l'épitre aux Romains a été étudiée à plusieurs reprises, soit à la Convention même, soit dans des livres ou des commentaires écrits dans la ligne de pensée de Keswick." Jean Marc Cruvellier, *L'Exégèse de Romains 7 et Le Mouvement de Keswick* (Amsterdam: Drukkerij Pasmans, 1961), p. 115.

45. Watchman Nee, *The Normal Christian Church Life,* rev. ed. (Washington, D.C.: International Students Press, 1969), p. 99.

46. Ibid., p. 8.

47. Ibid., p. 101.

48. Kinnear, *Against the Tide,* p. 126.

49. Chan, *My Uncle,* pp. 46-50.

50. Nee, *Church Life,* p. 75.

51. Nee, *Church Life,* pp. 50-52.

52. Chan, *My Uncle,* p. 50.

53. Lyall, *Mighty Men,* p. 85.

54. George N. Patterson, *Christianity in Communist China* (Waco, Texas: Word Books, 1969), pp. 38, 72-73, 79-80, 119, 134, 140-41. Mary Wang, *Stephen the Chinese Pastor* (London: Hodder & Stoughton, 1973), p. 98.

55. Wang, *Stephen,* p. 98.

56. Charles E. Notson, "Individualism Gone Astray: The 'Little Flock' of Watchman Ngnee," *The Alliance Weekly,* November 12, 1952, pp. 729-30. David M. Paton, *Christian Missions and the Judgement of God* (London: S.C.M., 1953), p. 49.

57. Notson, "Individualism," p. 730.

58. Paton, *Christian Missions,* p. 49.

59. Miss Helen Willis, quoted by Patterson, *Christianity,* p. 44.

60. Kinnear, *Against the Tide,* p. 154.

61. Cheung, *Ecclesiology,* p. 161.

62. Kinnear, *Against the Tide,* p. 146.

63. Ibid., p. 155.

64. *Tien Feng Magazine,*February 6, 1956, cited by *China Bulletin* 6, no. 6 (March 19, 1956):2.

65. Kinnear, *Against the Tide,* p. 177.

66. Harold G. King, "How I Kept Strong in Faith in a Communist Prison," *The Watchtower,* July 15, 1963, pp. 437-39.

67. Lyall, *Mighty Men,* p. 92.

68. Watchman Nee, *Further Talks on the Church Life* (Taipei: Gospel Book Room, 1968), p. 160.

69. Burton Crane, "Evangelist Drive Sweeps Formosa," *New York Times,* October 8, 1950, p. 11.

70. Hollenweger, *The Pentecostals,* pp. 6-7.

71. Stephen Kaung, *The Song of Degrees* (New York: Christian Fellowship Publishers, 1970), p. 103.

72. Stephen Kaung, *The Splendor of His Ways* (New York: Christian Fellowship Publishers, Inc., 1974), pp. 82-83.

73. Ibid., p. 88.

74. Ibid., p. 96.

75. Ibid., pp. 116-18, 126.

76. Cheung, *Ecclesiology,* passim.

77. Ibid., pp. 38, 48-50, 85-86.

78. Ibid., pp. 151-73.

79. Lo Shan [Pseud.], "From 'The Case of Fraud in the Church': To See the Conspiracy of the Secret Organization, Part II," *Nan Pei Chi* 33 (February 16, 1973):44-46.

80. Lee's studies on human nature are contained in his books *The Economy of God* (Los Angeles: The Stream Publishers, 1968) and *The Parts of Man* (Los Angeles: The Stream Publishers, 1969).

81. Witness Lee, "The Indwelling Christ: The Indwelling Christ in Galatians, Part One," *The Stream* 13:1 (February 1975):3.

82. As he did in *The Economy of God,* p. 82.

83. Idem, *Christ vs. Religion* (Taipei: The Gospel Book Room, [1971]), p. 77.

84. Ibid., p. 101.

85. As described in FF. Bruce, "Interpretation (Biblical)," in *Baker's Dictionary of Theology,* ed. Everett F. Harrison (Grand Rapids: Baker Book House, 1973), pp. 291-93, and in A. Berkeley Mickelson's book, *Interpreting the Bible* (Grand Rapids: William B. Eerdmans Publishing Company, 1963), passim. In both writers objective concerns provide balance to the subjective concerns of exposition.

86. Lee, *Christ vs. Religion*, pp. 42-43.
87. Heinrich Schlier, " αἱρέομαι, αἵρεσις,..., " in *Theological Dictionary of the New Testament*, eds. Kittle, Gerhard and Freidrich, Gerhard 1:180-85 and M.R.W. Farrer, "Heresy," In *Baker's* p. 268.

Chapter 2

1. C.T. Chan's memoir contains a number of these editorials, particularly during the period between 1928-33. *My Uncle*, pp. 16-17, 20-24, 74-129.
2. D.S. Murray, "The Church in Village Communities: I. Twenty Years Experience in Northern China," *International Review of Missions* 7 (1918):371.
3. Angus Kinnear to Dana Roberts, April 17, 1975, personal letter.
4. Nee, *Christian Life*, pp. 31-32.
5. Nee, *Twelve Baskets* 2:83-84.
6. Nee, *The Ministry*, pp. 134-35.
7. Nee, *Testimony*, p. 16.
8. F. Ernest Stoeffler's *The Rise of Evangelical Pietism* (Leiden: E.J. Brill, 1965) clearly shows that pietism was a strong influence upon the minds of evangelical leaders in England during the eighteenth and nineteenth century. The Keswick "Higher Life" Movement and Brethren groups were further influenced by their association with continental pietists: Keswick, through its close kinship with German Gemeinschaftsbewegung (Fellowship Movement); Brethrenism, through J.N. Darby's association with French pietism and George Müller's reading of the works of German Pietist August Hermann Francke (1663-1727). Donald Bloesch, *The Evangelical Renaissance* (Grand Rapids: William B. Eerdmans Publishing Company, 1973), p. 104; F. Roy Coad, *History of the Brethren Movement* (Grand Rapids: William B. Eerdmans Publishing Company, 1968), pp. 45, 48; B.B. Warfield, *Perfectionism*, ed. Samuel G. Craig (Philadelphia: Presbyterian and Reformed Publishing Company, 1971), pp. 312-48.
9. H.H. Rowley, "The Interpretation of the Song of Songs," *Journal of Theological Studies* 38 (1937): 350-51.
10. Nee, *Church Life*, p. 12.
11. Idem, *Christian Life*, back cover.
12. Enroth, Ericson and Peters, *The Jesus People*, p. 169.
13. Nee, *Love Not the World*, (Fort Washington, Pa.: Christian Literature Crusade, 1968), p. 14.
14. Ibid., p. 85.
15. Ibid., p. 86.
16. 1 Cor. 7:20.
17. Watchman Nee, *Christ the Sum of All Spiritual Things*, [trans. Stephen Kaung] (New York: Christian Fellowship Publishers, Inc., 1973), p. 59.

18. Witness Lee, *The Economy of God,* pp. 10-11. Alan Wallerstedt, Spiritual Counterfeits Project, personal letter.

19. Watchman Nee, *Changed into His Likeness* (Fort Washington, Pa.: Christian Literature Crusade, 1967).

20. Idem, *God's Work* (New York: Christian Fellowship Publishers, Inc., 1974). The book was produced from Miss Fischbacher's notes of a seminar given between June 11 and June 18, 1940.

21. Ibid., p. 27.

22. Ibid., p. 55.

23. Ibid.

24. Idem, *The Prayer Ministry of the Church* (New York: Christian Fellowship Publishers, Inc., 1973).

25. As found in C.I. Scofield's *Reference Bible* (New York: Oxford University Press, 1909), pp. 1332-34.

26. Nee, *Orthodoxy,* p. 69.

27. The series is published by Christian Fellowship Publishers (New York) and includes *A Living Sacrifice* (1972), *The Good Confession* (1973), *Assembling Together* (1973), *Not I but Christ* (1974), *Do All to the Glory of God* (1974) and *Love One Another* (1975).

28. Nee, *Not I, But Christ,* p. 135.

29. Idem, *Spiritual Man,* 1:17 ff.

30. Idem, *The Ministry of God's Word* (New York: Christian Fellowship Publishers, 1971), p. 15.

31. See pp. 148 ff.

32. See idem, *The Normal Christian Worker* (Hong Kong: Hong Kong Church Book Room, 1965), pp. 16, 133.

33. Nee, *Spiritual Reality,* p. 6.

Chapter 3

1. Karl Barth, *Church Dogmatics,* 4 vols., gen. eds. G.W. Bromily and T.F. Torrance (Edinburgh: T. and T. Clark, 1936-62), vol. 1: *The Doctrine of the Word of God: Prolegomena to Church Dogmatics,* 2 Parts (1936, 1956), trans. G.T. Thomson and H. Knight, 2:528ff.

2. Ibid., 1:98-140.

3. Nee, *The Ministry,* p. 11.

4. Ibid., p. 14.

5. Barth, *Doctrine of the Word,* 2:528ff.

6. Ibid., 1:123ff.

7. Nee, *Living Sacrifice,* p. 67.

8. Nee, *Search,* p. 12.

9. Ibid., p. 13.

10. 1 Cor. 2:13. See Nee, *Search, pp. 17-23.*

11. Nee, *The Ministry*, pp. 83-84.

12. Idem, *Search*, p. 15.

13. Idem, *The Ministry*, p. 60.

14. Idem, *Search*, p. 20.

15. Arthur T. Pierson, *The Bible and Spiritual Criticism*, reprint ed. (Grand Rapids: Baker Book House Company, 1970), p. 15.

16. Nee, *Search*, pp. 43-90.

17. See pp. 148ff. below.

18. Nee, *The Ministry*, p. 115.

19. Ibid., p. 103.

20. Idem, *Sit, Walk, Stand*, 4th ed., rev. (Fort Washington, Pa.: Christian Literature Crusade, 1962), p. 11. Cf. idem, *Christian Life*, pp. 40ff.

21. Idem, *The Ministry*, p. 124.

22. Idem, *Spiritual Man*, 2:10ff.; *The Ministry*, p. 131.

23. Idem, *Spiritual Man*, 1:28; *Gospel Dialogue* (New York: Christian Fellowship Publishers, 1975), pp. 106-9.

24. Idem, *Spiritual Knowledge* (New York: Christian Fellowship Publishers, Inc., 1973), pp. 65-82; *The Ministry*, pp. 143-45; *Christ: The Sum*, pp. 47-54; *God's Work* (New York: Christian Fellowship Publishers, 1974), pp. 17-24. See John 8:12 and other passages on "light."

25. Idem, *The Ministry*, p. 143.

26. Ibid., p. 144.

27. Idem, *The Spiritual Man*, 3:64-65.

28. Idem, *The Ministry*, p. 146.

29. Idem, *Knowledge*, p. 11.

30. Idem, *The Ministry*, p. 151; see also pp. 28, 29, 33, 39, 109, 146, 150-56, 180, 213, 218, 223-25, 263, and 266.

31. Ibid., p. 159. The word is incorrectly transliterated as "massam" in the English translation.

32. Ibid., p. 170.

33. Ibid., pp. 180-81.

34. Ibid., pp. 197ff. Cf. John 14:26.

35. Ibid., p. 208.

36. Ibid., p. 220.

37. Ibid., p. 227.

38. Ibid., pp. 245ff.

39. Ibid., p. 246.

40. Ibid., p. 281.

41. Ibid., p. 45.

42. Lee, *Christ vs. Religion*, pp. 32-33.

Chapter 4

1. C. Ryder Smith, *The Biblical Doctrine of Man* (London: The Epworth Press, 1951), passim.

2. Nee, *Spiritual Man*, 1:7.

3. Tertullian's *De Anima* is dichotomous. Origen's *De Principiis* supports a trichotomy.

4. See Warfield, *Perfectionism*, pp. 216-311.

5. See Jean Marc Etienne Cruvellier, *L'Exégèse de Romains 7 et Le Mouvement de Keswick* (S-Gravenhage: Vrije Universiteit te Amsterdam, 1961).

6. Rev. J.B. Heard, *The Tripartite Nature of Man* (Edinburgh: T. & T. Clark, 1875). Mary E. McDonough, *God's Plan of Redemption* (Boston: Hamilton Brothers, 1922). Andrew Murray, *The Spirit of Christ* (Fort Washington, Pa.: Christian Literature Crusade, 1963). G.H. Pember, *Earth's Earliest Ages* (Old Tappan, N.J.: Fleming H. Revell Company, n.d.). Jessie Penn-Lewis, *Soul and Spirit: A Glimpse into Bible Psychology* (Dorset, England: The Overcomer Literature Trust, n.d.). Delavan Leonard Pierson, *Arthur T. Pierson* (New York: Fleming H. Revell Company, 1912), p. 283.

7. Nee, *Spiritual Man*, 1:21-22.

8. Ibid., 1:22.

9. Ibid., p. 23; idem, *The Release of the Spirit* (Indianapolis: Premium Literature Co., 1965), p. 29.

10. Heard, *Tripartite Nature*, pp. 39-49; McDonough, *Plan*, pp. 21-22; Pember, *Ages*, pp. 103-16; Penn-Lewis, *Soul*, p. 4; Rev. C.I. Scofield, gen. ed., *The Scofield Reference Bible*, 2nd ed. (New York: Oxford University Press, 1917), loc. cit. (A. T. Pierson is listed here as a consulting editor).

11. Nee, *Spiritual Man*, 1:23-26; idem, *Latent Power*, pp. 10-11; idem, *Christian Life*, pp. 155-56.

12. Idem, *Spiritual Man*, 1:24; cf. *Knowledge*, p. 85.

13. Ibid., pp. 26-28.

14. Ibid., p. 26.

15. *exō/exōthen:* Matt. 23:27, 28; 2 Cor. 4:16; 1 Pet. 3:3. *esō/esōthen:* Luke 11:39; Rom. 7:22; Eph. 3:16.

16. Taken from McDonough, *Plan*, p. viii.

17. Nee, *Latent Power*, p. 15.

18. Idem, *Spiritual Man*, 1:44; 3:158.

19. Ibid., 1:43.

20. Idem, *Christian Life*, p. 80.

21. Ibid., p. 81.

22. Idem, *Spiritual Man*, 1:46.

23. Ibid., p. 47.

24. Ibid., p. 50.

25. Idem, *Christian Life*, pp. 110-11.

26. Nee, *Spiritual Man*, 1:31-41.

27. See Nee, *Spiritual Man*, 1:35.

28. Ibid., p. 34.

29. Ibid., pp. 7-20.

30. Ibid., pp. 29-30.

31. Ibid., p. 55.

32. Ibid., pp. 57-60.

33. William L. Lane, *The Gospel According to Mark: The English Text with Introduction, Exposition and Notes*, The New International Commentary on the New Testament (Grand Rapids: William B. Eerdmans Publishing Company, 1974), p. 564.

34. Nee, *Spiritual Man*, 1:60; idem, *Christian Life*, passim; idem, *Living Sacrifice*, pp. 14-17; idem, *Not I, But Christ*, pp. 114-20; idem, *Gospel Dialogue* (New York: Christian Fellowship Publishers, 1975), pp. 67, 98.

35. Andrew Murray, *The Spirit of Christ*, pp. 14-16; Nee, *Not I, But Christ*, p. 132.

36. Nee, *Christian Life*, pp. 141-44.

37. Idem, *Christ the Sum*, p. 59.

38. Ibid.

39. Idem, *Spiritual Man*, 2:10-14.

40. Ibid., 2:10.

41. Ibid., p. 26.

42. Ibid., pp. 67-70.

43. Ibid., p. 69.

44. Nee, *Spiritual Man*, 2:70.

45. 1 John 2:20, 27 RSV; Nee, *Spiritual Man*, 2:73.

46. Ibid., p. 75.

47. Ibid., pp. 57-76.

48. Ibid., p. 77.

49. See pp. 65ff.

50. Nee, *Spiritual Man*, 2:77.

51. Ibid., p. 78.

52. Ibid., p. 80.

53. Ibid.

54. Ibid., p. 88.

55. Ibid., pp. 52-55, 58.

56. Idem, *Prayer Ministry*, p. 17.

57. Idem, *Spiritual Man*, 2:107.

58. Ibid., p. 111.

59. Ibid., p. 118.

60. Ibid., p. 123. Cf. John Wesley, *Wesley's Standard Sermons*, 2 vols., ed. Edward H. Sugden (Nashville: Lamar & Barton, n.d.), 1:121; idem, *The Works of John Wesley*, 14 vols., ed. Thomas Jackson, reprint ed. (Kansas City, Mo.: Nazarene Publishing House, n.d.), 10: 394-406.

61. Nee, *Spiritual Man*, 2:122-25.

62. Ibid., p. 68.

63. Ibid., pp. 145-46.
64. Ibid., p. 146.
65. Ibid., pp. 146-48.
66. Ibid., pp. 148-50.
67. Ibid., p. 150.
68. Ibid.
69. Ibid., pp. 151-53.
70. Ibid., p. 151.
71. Ibid., 3:153-56.
72. Ibid., 2:156-58.
73. Ibid., pp. 156-157.
74. Ibid.
75. Ibid., pp. 158-60.
76. Ibid., p. 160.
77. Ibid.
78. Ibid.
79. Ibid., p. 180.
80. Ibid., p. 176.
81. Ibid., 1:26; idem, *Release*, pp. 10-12; *Knowledge*, p. 85. Here the relationship is most explicitly stated.
82. Nee, *Spiritual Man*, 1:144-78; *Latent Power*, pp. 32-36, 45-56, 64-80; *Christian Life*, pp. 158-63; *Spiritual Reality*, pp. 10-64.
83. Idem, *Spiritual Man*, 2:191.
84. Ibid., p. 190.
85. Ibid., p. 194.
86. Ibid., p. 196.
87. Ibid., pp. 202-11; *Christian Life*, p. 174.
88. Nee, *Spiritual Man*, 2:202.
89. Ibid., p. 211.
90. Ibid., p. 212.
91. Ibid., p. 222.
92. Idem, *Knowledge*, p. 91.
93. For an understanding of the prescientific, mythopoetic mind of the Bible writers, see H. and H.A. Frankfort, John H. Wilson and Thorkild Jacobsen, *Before Philosophy: The Intellectual Adventure of Ancient Man* (Baltimore: Penguin Books, 1951), pp. 137-234.
94. Heard, *Tripartite Nature*, p. 52.
95. Nee, *Spiritual Man*, 3:7.
96. Ibid., 3:8.
97. Ibid., pp. 7-8.
98. Ibid., pp.9-10.
99. Ibid., p. 12.
100. Idem, *Knowledge*, p. 86.
101. Idem, *Spiritual Man*, 3:14.

102. Ibid., p. 27.

103. Ibid., pp. 18-27.

104. Ibid., p. 28.

105. Ibid.

106. Idem, *Knowledge,* pp. 119ff.

107. Idem, *Spiritual Man,* 3:163-70.

108. See p. 79ff.

109. Idem, *Dialogue,* pp. 106-8; idem, *Spiritual Man,* 2:75-77.

110. Idem, *Spiritual Man,* 3:77.

111. Ibid., p. 95.

112. Ibid., p. 78.

113. Ibid., pp. 78-79; idem, *Dialogue,* pp. 106-7.

114. Idem, *Spiritual Man,* 3:85.

115. Ibid., pp. 91-92.

116. Penn-Lewis and Evans, *War,* pp. 69-70, quoted in Nee, *Spiritual Man,* 3:93.

117. Nee, *Spiritual Man* 3:98.

118. Ibid., p. 97.

119. Ibid., pp. 104-7.

120. Ibid., pp. 109-18.

121. Ibid., p. 123.

122. Ibid., pp. 125-36.

123. Idem, *Latent Power,* p. 8.

124. David K. Jordon, *Gods, Ghosts, and Ancestors: The Folk Religion of a Taiwanese Village* (Los Angeles: University of California Press, 1972), p. 74.

125. Nee, *Latent Power,* pp. 32ff.

126. Idem, *Release,* pp. 66-67.

127. Idem, *Latent Power,* pp. 85-86.

128. John Murray, *The Epistle to the Romans,* The New International Commentary on the New Testament (Grand Rapids: William B. Eerdmans Publishing Company, 1965), p. 292.

129. Nee, *Spiritual Man,* 3:143.

130. See ibid., pp. 168-73.

131. Ibid., pp. 148ff.

132. Ibid., pp. 183-84; cf. Isa. 53:4-5.

133. Nee, *Spiritual Man,* 3:161ff.

134. Ibid., pp. 158-95.

135. Ibid., pp. 166-67.

136. Ibid., p. 218.

137. Ibid.

138. Bernard Erling, "The Story of Watchman Nee," *Lutheran Quarterly* 28 (May 1976):140-55. Kinnear, *Against the Tide.* Carl F.H. Henry, "Footnotes: Watchman Nee," *Christianity Today,* May 9, 1975, pp. 31-32. Lyall, *Mighty Men.*

139. Nee, *Christian Life,* p. 141.

140. Idem, *Sit,* passim.

141. Idem, *Christian Life,* pp. 9-22; *Living Sacrifice,* pp. 3-14; *Spiritual Man* 1:55-82.

142. E.g., Leon Morris, *The Apostolic Preaching of the Cross* (Grand Rapids: William B. Eerdmans Company, 1955), pp. 108-24; *TDNT* 1, 175, 18.

143. Nee, *Spiritual Man,* 1:61.

144. Idem, *Christian Life,* p. 16. See idem *Spiritual Man,* 1:76.

145. Idem, *Spiritual Man,* 1:77-82; idem, *Christian Life,* p. 24.

146. Idem, *Spiritual Man,* p. 133.

147. Rom. 6:6. Quoted in Nee, *Christian Life,* p. 40; idem, *Spiritual Man,* 1:78.

148. Rom. 6:11. See Nee, *Christian Life,* pp. 45-60; idem, *Spiritual Man* 1:137, 199.

149. Ibid., p. 135.

150. Idem, *Living Sacrifice,* pp. 51-66; idem, *Christian Life,* pp. 70-75.

151. Idem, *Living Sacrifice,* pp. 52-53.

152. Idem, *Christian Life,* p. 73.

153. Ibid., p. 71.

154. Ibid., 74-75; idem, *Living Sacrifice,* p. 62.

155. Ibid.

156. Idem, *Christian Life,* pp. 143f.

157. Ibid., pp. 76-85; idem, *Spiritual Man,* 1:44-46.

158. Idem, *Christian Life,* p. 80.

159. See pp. 38-40 supra.

160. On traditional Pentecostal theology see Hollenweger, *The Pentecostals,* pp. 321-52; Frederic Dale Bruner, *A Theology of the Holy Spirit* (Grand Rapids: William B. Eerdmans Publishing Company, 1970), passim; and Ralph M. Riggs, *The Spirit Himself* (Springfield, Mo.: Gospel Publishing Company, 1949), passim. For a Neo-Pentecostal approach see Howard M. Ervin, *These Are Not Drunken as Ye Suppose* (Plainfield, N.J.: Logos International, 1968), passim; Charles E. Hummel, *Fire in the Fireplace: Contemporary Charismatic Renewal* (Downers Grove, Ill.: Inter-Varsity Press, 1978), pp. 53-190; and Thomas A. Small, *Reflected Glory: The Spirit in Christ and Christians* (Grand Rapids: William B. Eerdmans Publishing Company, 1975), pp. 76-103. For a brief survey of both theologies see Russel Spittler, ed., *Perspectives on the New Pentecostalism* (Grand Rapids: Baker Book House, 1976), pp. 57-104.

161. Nee, *Christian Life,* pp. 87-92.

162. Ibid., pp. 95-97.

163. Ibid., pp. 94, 97.

164. Ibid., p. 101.

165. Ibid.
166. Ibid., pp. 106-121.
167. Quoted in ibid., p. 108.
168. Ibid., p. 114.
169. Gal. 2:20, quoted in ibid., p. 9.
170. Idem, *Spiritual Man,* 1:103.
171. Ibid., 2:246.
172. Ibid., 3:41.
173. Ibid., p. 132.
174. Ibid., p. 217.
175. Nee, *Release,* pp. 14-15.
176. Idem, *Living Sacrifice,* pp. 67-82; idem, *Search,* passim.
177. Idem, *Ministry* passim.
178. Idem, *Living Sacrifice,* pp. 83-97; idem., *Prayer Ministry,* passim.
179. Idem, *Living Sacrifice,* pp. 99-115.
180. Idem, *Do All to the Glory of God,* Basic Lesson series, vol. 3 [trans., Stephen Kaung.] (New York: Christian Fellowship Publishers, Inc., 1974), pp. 1-45.
181. Idem, *Good Confession,* pp. 97-114.
182. Ibid., pp. 55-96.
183. Ibid., pp. 15-33; idem, *Love Not,* passim.
184. Idem, *Do All,* pp. 197-214.
185. Ibid., pp. 153-174.
186. See chapter 5.

Chapter 5

1. Kinnear, *Against the Tide,* pp. 34, 56.
2. Nee, *Testimony,* p. 31.
3. C.H. Mackintosh, *The Assembly of God,* pp. 35ff. Quoted in William Reid, *Plymouth Brethrenism: Unveiled and Refuted* (Edinburgh: William Oliphant & Company, 1880), p. 57.
4. Nee, *Assembly,* pp. 33-42.
5. Idem, *Church Life,* pp. 65-71.
6. Lee, *Christ vs. Religion,* passim.
7. Allen J. Swanson, *Taiwan: Mainline versus Independent Church Growth: A Study in Contrasts* (S. Pasedena, Cal.: William Carey Library, 1970), pp. 16-64.
8. Lyall, *Mighty Men,* passim.
9. Nee, *Further Talks,* pp. 96ff.
10. Nee, *What Shall This Man Do?* (Fort Washington, Pa.: Christian Literature Crusade, 1961), p. 71.
11. Ibid., p. 77.

12. Idem, *Christ the Sum*, p. 59; idem, *Love One Another*, p. 194.

13. Idem, *The Glorious Church*, pp. 27-45.

14. Ibid., pp. 31ff.

15. Nee, *Church Life*, pp. 47-49.

16. Ibid., pp. 56-57.

17. Ibid., pp. 64-71.

18. Ibid., p. 41.

19. Ibid., p. 75.

20. Idem, *The Glorious Church*, pp. 31ff.

21. Kinnear, *Against the Tide*, p. 131.

22. Kinnear, *Against the Tide*, pp. 55-58; Lo-Shan [pseud.], "From 'The Case of Fraud in the Church': To See the Conspiracy of the Church at the Secret Organization, Part One," *Nan Pei Chi* 32 (January 16, 1973):37.

23. Nee, *Orthodoxy*, p. 14.

24. Ibid., p. 101.

25. Idem, *Further Talks*, p. 155.

26. Ibid., pp. 159-62.

27. Ibid., p. 159.

28. Kinnear, *Against the Tide*, p. 138; Cheung, *Ecclesiology*, p. 26; Lo-Shan [pseud.]. "From 'The Case of Fraud in the Church': To See the Conspiracy of the Church by the Secret Organization, Part Three," *Nan Pei Chi* 34 (March 10, 1973):58-59.

29. Watchman Nee, *Spiritual Authority* (New York: Christian Fellowship Publishers, 1972), p. 67.

30. Kinnear, *Against the Tide*, p. 139.

31. Nee, *Authority*, p. 71.

32. Idem, *"Come"*, p. 208.

33. Ibid., pp. 153-57.

34. Idem, *Love Not*, p. 86.

35. Idem, *God's Plan and the Overcomers* (New York: Christian Fellowship Publishers, 1977), p. 82. Cf. Idem, *Gospel Dialogue*, pp. 58, 88-89.

36. Idem, *Gospel Dialogue*, p. 157.

37. Idem, *God's Plan*, p. 61.

38. Idem, *"Come"*, p. 62.

Chapter 6

1. Nee, *Spiritual Man*, 1:11.

Bibliography

The Writings of Watchman Nee

Assembly Together. Basic Lessons Series, vol. 3. [Translated by Stephen Kaung.] New York: Christian Fellowship Publishers, Inc., 1973.

The Body of Christ. Los Angeles: The Stream Publishers, n.d. [booklet].

The Body of Christ: A Reality. New York Christian Fellowship Publishers, 1978.

Burden and Prayer. Taiwan: The Stream, n.d. [booklet].

Changed into His Likeness. Fort Washington, Pa.: Christian Literature Crusade.

Christ: The Sum of All Spiritual Things. [Translated by Stephen Kaung.] New York: Christian Fellowship Publishers, 1973.

Come, Lord Jesus. New York: Christian Fellowship Publishers, 1976.

Do All to the Glory of God. Basic Lesson Series, vol. 5. New York: Christian Fellowship Publishers, 1974.

Further Talks on the Church Life. Taipei: The Gospel Book Room, 1968.

The Glorious Church. Taipei: The Gospel Book Room, 1968.

The Glory of His Life. New York: Christian Fellowship Publishers, 1976.

God's Plan and the Overcomers. New York: Christian Fellowship Publishers, 1977.

God's Work. New York: Christian Fellowship Publishers, Inc., 1974.

The Good Confession. Basic Lesson Series, vol. 2. [Translated by Stephen Kaung.] New York: Christian Fellowship Publishers, Inc., 1973.

Gospel Dialogue. New York: Christian Fellowship Publishers, 1975.

The Latent Power of the Soul. [Translated by Stephen Kaung.] New York: Christian Fellowship Publishers, Inc., 1972.

A Living Sacrifice. Basic Lesson Series, vol. 1. [Translated by Stephen Kaung.] New York: Christian Fellowship Publishers, Inc., 1972.

Love Not the World. Edited by Angus I. Kinnear. Fort Washington, Pa.: Christian Literature Crusade, 1968.

Love One Another. Basic Lesson Series, vol. 6. [Translated by Stephen Kaung.] New York: Christian Fellowship Publishers, Inc., 1975.

The Ministry of God's Word. [Translated by Stephen Kaung.] New York: Christian Fellowship Publishers, Inc., 1971.

Ministry to the House or to the Lord. Los Angeles: The Stream Publishers, n.d.

The Normal Christian Church Life. Rev. ed. Washington: International Students Press, 1969.

The Normal Christian Life. Edited by Angus Kinnear. 3rd ed. Fort Washington, Pa.: Christian Literature Crusade, 1961.

The Normal Christian Worker. Hong Kong: Hong Kong Church Book Room, 1965.

Not I, But Christ. Basic Lesson Series, vol. 4. [Translated by Stephen Kaung.] New York: Christian Fellowship Publishers, Inc., 1974.

The Orthodoxy of the Church. Los Angeles: The Stream Publishers, 1970.

Practical Issues of This Life. New York: Christian Fellowship Publishers, 1975.

The Prayer Ministry of the Church. [Translated by Stephen

Kaung.] New York: Christian Fellowship Publishers, Inc., 1973.

The Release of the Spirit. Indianapolis: Premium Literature Co., 1965.

Sit, Walk, Stand. 4th ed., rev. Fort Washington, Pa.: Christian Literature Crusade, 1962.

Song of Songs. Translated by Elizabeth K. Mei and Daniel Smith. Fort Washington, Pa.: Christian Literature Crusade, 1965.

Spiritual Authority. [Translated by Stephen Kaung.] New York: Christian Fellowship Publishers, Inc., 1972.

Spiritual Knowledge. [Translated by Stephen Kaung.] New York: Christian Fellowship Publishers, Inc., 1973.

The Spiritual Man. 3 vols. [Translated by Stephen Kaung.] New York: Christian Fellowship Publishers, Inc. 1968.

Spiritual Reality or Obsession. [Translated by Stephen Kaung.] New York: Christian Fellowship Publishers, Inc., 1970.

A Table in the Wilderness. Edited by Angus I. Kinnear. Fort Washington, Pa.: Christian Literature Crusade, 1965.

Twelve Baskets Full. 3 vols. Hong Kong: Hong Kong Church Book Room Ltd., 1965.

Twelve Baskets Full. Vol. 4. Hong Kong: Hong Kong Church Book Room, 1975.

What Shall This Man Do? Edited by Angus I. Kinnear. Fort Washington, Pa.: Christian Literature Crusade, 1961.

Ye Search the Scriptures. [Translated by Stephen Kaung.] New York: Christian Fellowship Publishers, Inc., 1974.

Watchman Nee's Testimony. Compiled by K.H. Weigh. Hong Kong: Church Book Room, 1974.

Works on Watchman Nee
Chan, Stephen C.T. *Wo Ti Kau Fu Ni To Sheng* [My Uncle Watchman Nee]. Hong Kong: Alliance Press, 1970.

Chen, James. *Meet Brother Nee*. Hong Kong: The Christian Publishers, 1976.

Cheung, James Mo-Oi. *The Ecclesiology of Watchman Nee and Witness Lee*. Fort Washington, Pa.: Christian Literature Crusade, 1972.

Erling, Bernard. "The Story of Watchman Nee." *Lutheran Quarterly* 28(May 1976):140-55.

Henry, Carl F.H. "Footnotes: Watchman Nee." *Christianity Today*, May 9, 1975, pp. 31-32.

Kang-Shui [pseud.]. "The Case of Fraud in the Church: The Name of God Should Not Be Blasphemed." *Nan Pei Chi* 27 (Aug. 16, 1972):9-10.

Kinnear, Angus I. *The Story of Watchman Nee: Against the Tide*. Fort Washington, Pa.: Christian Literature Crusade, 1973.

Lo-Shan [pseud.]. "From 'The Case of Fraud in the Church': To See the Conspiracy of the Church by the Secret Organization, Part One." *Nan Pei Chi* 32 (January 16, 1973):37-39.

________. "From 'The Case of Fraud in the Church': To See the Conspiracy of the Church by the Secret Organization, Part Two." *Nan Pei Chi* 33 (February 16, 1973):44-46.

________. "From 'The Case of Fraud in the Church': To See the Conspiracy of the Church by the Secret Organization, Part Three." *Nan Pei Chi* 34 (March 10, 1973):56-60.

Lyall, Leslie. *Three of China's Mighty Men*. London: Overseas Missionary Fellowship, 1973.

Sources Consulted: Books

Alford, Henry. *The Greek Testament: With a Critically Revised Text: A Digest of Various Readings: Marginal References to Verbal and Idiomatic Usage; Prolegomena: And a Critical and Exegetical Commentary*. 4 vols. Boston: Lee and Shepard, 1888.

Allen, Roland. *The Ministry of the Spirit: Selected Writings of Roland Allen.* Reprint ed. Edited by David M. Paton. Grand Rapids: William B. Eerdmans Publishing Co., 1962.

__________. *Missionary Methods: St. Paul's Or Ours?* Grand Rapids: William B. Eerdmans Publishing Co., 1962.

__________. *The Spontaneous Expansion of the Church.* Grand Rapids: William B. Eerdmans Publishing Co., 1962.

Barabas, Steven. *So Great Salvation: The History of the Keswick Convention.* London: Marshall, Morgan and Scott, 1952.

Bardstra, Andrew. *The Law and the Elements of the World: An Exegetical Study in Aspects of Paul's Teaching.* Grand Rapids: William B. Eerdmans Publishing Co., 1964.

Barr, Pat. *To China with Love.* Garden City, New York: Doubleday & Co., 1973.

Barth, Karl. *Church Dogmatics.* 4 vols. Edited by G.W. Bromily and T.F. Torrance. Edinburgh: T. & T. Clark, 1936-62.

Berton, Pierre. *The Comfortable Pew.* Philadelphia: J.B. Lippencott Company, 1965.

Blanford, Carl E. *Chinese Churches in Thailand.* Bangkok: Suriyaban Publishers, n.d.

Bloesch, Donald. *The Evangelical Renaissance.* Grand Rapids: William B. Eerdmans Publishing Co., 1973.

Boyd, Forrest. *Instant Analysis: Confessions of a White House Correspondent.* Atlanta: John Knox Press, 1974.

Bugh, Richard C., Jr. *Religion in Communist China.* Nashville: Abington Press, 1970.

Bruner, Frederick Dale. *A Theology of the Holy Spirit.* Grand Rapids: William B. Eerdmans Publishing Co., 1970.

Butterworth, G.W., ed. *Origin On First Principles.* New York: Harper & Row, 1966.

Clennell, W.J. *The Historical Development of Religion in*

China. New York: E.P. Dutton & Co., 1917.

China Yearbook 1965-66. Taipei: China Publishing Company, 1966.

Coad, F. Roy. *A History of the Brethren Movement.* Exeter: The Paternoster Press, 1968.

Coates, C.A. *An Outline of the Song of Solomon.* Kingston-on-Thames, England: Stow Hill Bible and Tract Depot, n.d.

Cohen, Paul A. *China and Christianity: The Missionary Movement and Growth of Chinese Antiforeignism, 1860-1870.* Harvard East Asian Series, no. 11. Cambridge: Harvard University Press, 1963.

Colson, F.H. and Whitaker, G.H. *Philo.* 10 vols. The Loeb Classical Library. Cambridge: Harvard University Press, 1929.

Cruvellier, John Marc Etienne. *L'Exêgèse de Romains 7 et le Mouvement de Keswick.* Amsterdam: Drukkerij Pasmans, 1961.

Danielou, Jean, S.J. *From Shadows to Reality: Studies in the Typology of the Fathers.* Translated by Dom Wulstan Hillerd. London: Burnes & Oates, 1960.

Darby, J.N. *The Collected Writings of J.N. Darby.* 32 vols. Edited by William Kelly. London: G. Morrish, 1867-83.

Delitzsch, Franz. *A System of Biblical Psychology.* Edinburgh: T. & T. Clark, 1967.

Domes, Jurgen. *The International Politics of China, 1949-1972.* Translated by Rudiger Machetzki. New York: Praeger Publishers, 1973.

Douglas, Rev. W.M. *Andrew Murray and His Message: One of God's Choice Saints.* New York: Fleming H. Revell Co., n.d.

Ebon, Martin. *Lin Piao: The Life and Writings of China's New Ruler.* New York: Stein and Day, 1970.

Enroth, Ronald M.; Ericson, Edward E., Jr. and Peters, C. Breckinridge. *The Jesus People: Old Time Religion in the*

Age of Aquarius. Grand Rapids: William B. Eerdmans Publishing Co., 1972.

Evans, Eifion. *The Welsh Revival of 1904.* London: Evangelical Press, 1969.

Fenn, C.H. *The Five Thousand Dictionary.* Cambridge: Harvard University Press, 1963.

Forsyth, Sidney A. *An American Missionary Community in China, 1895-1905.* Harvard East Asian Monographs 43, Cambridge: East Asian Research Center, Harvard University, 1971.

Foster, Harry. *A Study Guide to Watchman Nee's "The Normal Christian Life."* Eastbourne, England: Victory Press, 1976.

Frankfort, H. and H.A.; Wilson, John H. and Jacobsen, Thorkild. *Before Philosophy: The Intellectual Adventure of Ancient Man.* Baltimore: Penguin Books, 1951.

Frodsham, Stanley H. *With Signs Following.* Springfield, Mo.: Gospel Publishing House, 1946.

Gelpi, Donald L. *Pentecostalism: A Theological Viewpoint.* New York: Paulist Press, 1971.

Giles, Herbert A. *A Chinese Biographical Dictionary.* Reprint ed. Taipei: Literature House, n.d.

Girard, Marcel, ed. *Nagel's Encyclopedia-Guide: China.* Geneva: Nagel Publications, 1968.

Goertz, Peter S. "A History of the Chinese Indigenous Christian Church under the American Board in Fukien Province." Ph.D. dissertation, Yale University, 1933.

Green, Michael. *I Believe in the Holy Spirit.* Grand Rapids: William B. Eerdmans Publishing Co., 1975.

Grubb, Violet M. *The Chinese Indigenous Church Movement.* London: World Dominion Press, n.d.

Guyon, Madame. *Autobiography of Madame Guyon.* Chicago: Moody Press, n.d.

Harford, John Battersby and MacDonald, Frederick Charles. *Handley Carr Glyn Moule.* London: Hodeer & Stoughton, 1922.

Harris, H.M. "Indigenous Churches in China." Ph.D. dissertation, Southern Baptist Theological Seminary, 1927.

Harrison, Everett F., ed. *Baker's Dictionary of Theology.* Grand Rapids: Baker Book House, 1973.

Harrison, John A. *China Since 1800.* New York: Harbinger Book, Harcourt, Brace & World, 1967.

Heard, Rev. J.B. *The Tripartite Nature of Man.* Edinburgh: T. & T. Clark, 1875.

Henry, Carl F.H. *Christian Personal Ethics.* Grand Rapids: William B. Eerdmans Publishing Co. 1957.

Hollenweger, Walter J. *The Pentecostals: The Charismatic Movement in the Churches.* Translated by R.A. Wilson. Minneapolis: Augsburg Publishing House, 1972.

Hopkins, Evan H. *The Law of Liberty in the Spiritual Life.* Philadelphia: The Sunday School Times, 1952.

Jamieson, Robert; Fausset, A.R.; and Brown, David. *Commentary, Critical and Explanatory on the Old and New Testaments.* 2 vols. Hartford: S.S. Scranton and Co., 1887.

Jewett, Robert. *Paul's Anthropological Terms: A Study of Their Use in Conflict Settings.* Arbeiten zur Geschichte des Antiken Judentums und des Urchristentums. Band 10. Leiden: E. J. Brill, 1971.

Jones, Francis Price. *The Church in Communist China: A Protestant Appraisal.* New York: Friendship Press, 1962.

Jordon, David K. *Gods, Ghosts, and Ancestors: The Folk Religion of a Taiwanese Village.* Los Angeles: University of California Press, 1972.

Kaung, Stephen. *The Song of Degrees.* New York: Christian Fellowship Publishers, Inc., 1970.

__________. *The Splendor of His Ways: Seeing the Lord's End in*

Job. New York: Christian Fellowship Publishers, 1974.

Keswick Convention Trustees. *The Keswick convention 1938.* London: Pickering & Inglis, 1938.

________. *The Keswick Week 1948.* London: Marshall, Morgan & Scott, 1948.

Kittel, Gerhard and Friedrich, Gerhard, eds. *Theological Dictionary of the New Testament.* 10 vols. translated by Geoffrey W. Bromiley. Grand Rapids: William B. Eerdmans Publishing Co. 1964-76.

Klein, Donald W. and Clark, Ann B. *Biographic Dictionary of Chinese Communism 1921-1965.* 2 vols. Cambridge: Harvard University Press, 1971.

Kummel, Werner Georg. *Romer 7 und Die Bekenhrung Des Paulus.* Leipzig: J.C. Hinrichs'sche Buchhandlung, 1929.

Ladd, George Eldon. *A Theology of the New Testament.* Grand Rapids: William B. Eerdmans Publishing Company, 1975.

Lane, William. *The Gospel According to Mark: The English Text with Introduction, Exposition and Notes.* The New International Commentary on the New Testament. Grand Rapids: William B. Eerdmans Publishing Company, 1974.

La Rondelle, Hans Karl. *Perfection and Perfectionism.* Amsterdam: J.H. Kok N.V. Kampen, 1971.

Latourette, Kenneth Scott. *The Chinese: Their History and Culture.* New York: Macmillan Co., 1962.

Lee, Witness. *The Baptism in the Holy Spirit.* Los Angeles: The Stream Publishers, 1969.

________. *Christ vs. Religion.* Taipei: The Gospel Book Room, [1971].

________. *The Economy of God.* Los Angeles: The Stream Publishers, 1968.

________. *The Four Major Steps of Christ.* Los Angeles: The Stream Publishers, 1969.

________. *The Parts of Man.* Los Angeles: The Stream Publishers, 1969.

Legge, James. *Christianity in China: Nestorianism, Roman Catholicism, Protestantism.* London: Trubner & Co., 1888.

Lyall, Leslie T. *Come Wind, Come Weather: The Present Experience of the Church in China.* Chicago: Moody Press, 1960.

________. *Red Sky at Night: Communism Confronts Christianity in China.* Chicago: Moody Press, 1969.

McDonough, Mary E. *God's Plan of Redemption.* Boston: Hamilton Brothers, 1922.

________. *The Story of Redemption.* Bournemouth, England: The "Overcomer" Bookroom, n.d.

Matthews, David. *I Saw the Welsh Revival.* Chicago: Moody Press, 1951.

Metcalfe, J.C. *In the Mould of the Cross: A Pen-Sketch of the Life and Ministry of Jessie Penn-Lewis.* Dorset, England: Overcomer Literature Trust, n.d.

Meyer, Heinrich August Wilhelm. *Critical and Exegetical Handbook to the Gospels of Mark and Luke.* Translated by Robert Ernest Wallis and William P. Dickson. Edinburgh: T. & T. Clark, 1883.

Michelson, A. Berkeley. *Interpreting the Bible.* Grand Rapids: William B. Eerdmans Publishing Co., 1963.

Minnear, Paul S. *Horizons of Christian Community.* St. Louis, Mo.: The Bethany Press, 1959.

Morgan, G. Campbell and Stead, W.T. *The Welsh Revival.* Boston: The Pilgrim Press, 1905.

Moule, Handley C.G. *Outline of Christian Doctrine.* London: Hodder & Stoughton, 1902.

Murray, Andrew. *The Spirit of Christ.* Fort Washington, Pa.: Christian Literature Crusade, 1963.

Murray, John. *The Epistle to the Romans, The New Interna-

tional Commentary on the New Testament. Grand Rapids: William B. Eerdmans Publishing Co., 1968.

National Council of Churches of Christ in the U.S.A. *Documents of the Three-Self Movement: Source Materials for the Study of the Protestant Church in Communist China.* New York: Far Eastern Office, Division of Foreign Missions, 1963.

Newham, Richard. *About Chinese.* Baltimore: Penguin Books, 1971.

Niebuhr, Reinhold. *The Nature and Destiny of Man.* New York: Charles Scribner's Sons, 1949.

Pakenham-Walsh, W.S. *Twenty Years in China.* Cambridge: W. Heffer & Sons, 1935.

Palmer, Edwin H. *The Five Points of Calvinism.* Grand Rapids: Baker Book House, 1972.

__________. *The Person and Ministry of the Holy Spirit: The Traditional Calvinistic Perspective.* Grand Rapids: Baker Book House, 1974.

Paton, David M. *Christian Missions and the Judgement of God.* London: S.C.M. Press, 1953.

__________. ed. *Reform of the Ministry: A Study in the Work of Roland Allen.* London: Lutterworth Press, 1968.

Patterson, George N. *Christianity in Communist China.* Waco, Texas: Word Books, 1969.

Paxson, Ruth. *Called unto Holiness.* Grand Rapids: Zondervan Publishing House, n.d.

__________. *Life of the Highest Plane.* 3 vols. New York: Fleming H. Revell Co., 1928.

Pember, G.H. *Earth's Earliest Ages.* Old Tappan, N.J.: Fleming H. Revell Co., n.d.

Penn-Lewis, Jessie. *The Awakening in Wales.* Dorset, England: The Overcomer Literature Trust, n.d.

__________. *The Centrality of the Cross.* Dorset, England: The Overcomer Literature Trust, n.d.

__________. *The Cross of Calvary.* Dorset, England: The Overcomer

Literature Trust, n.d.

————. *Life in the Spirit*. Dorset, England: The Overcomer Literature Trust, n.d.

————. *Life out of Death*. Dorset, England: The Overcomer Literature Trust, n.d.

————. *Soul and Spirit: A Glimpse into Bible Psychology*. Dorset England: The Overcomer Literature Trust, n.d.

————. *The Spiritual Warfare*. Dorset, England: The Overcomer Literature Trust, n.d.

————. *The Hidden Ones*. Dorset, England: The Overcomer Literature Trust, n.d.

————. and Roberts, Evan. *War on the Saints*. Dorset, England: The Overcomer Literature Trust, n.d.

Philip, Robert. *Peace with China! or, The Crisis of Christianity in Central Asia: A Letter to the Right Honourable T.B. Macauly, Secretary of War*. London: John Snow, 1840.

Pierson, Arthur T. *The Bible and Spiritual Criticism*. Reprint ed. Grand Rapids: Baker Book House, 1970.

————. *Forward Movements of the Last Half Century*. New York: Funk & Wagnalls Co., 1905.

Pierson, Delavan Leonard. *Arthur T. Pierson*. New York: Fleming H. Revell Co., 1912.

Pollock, John C. *The Keswick Story*. London: Hodeer & Stoughton, 1964.

Reid, William. *Plymouth Brethrenism: Unveiled and Refuted*. Edinburgh: William Oliphant & Co., 1880.

Ridderbos, Herman. *Paul: An Outline of His Theology*. Translated by Richard de Witt. Grand Rapids: William B. Eerdmans Publishing Co., 1975.

Robinson, H. Wheeler. *The Christian Doctrine of Man*. 3rd ed. Edinburgh: T. & T. Clark, 1926.

Sandeen, Ernest R. *The Origins of Fundamentalism*. Facet Books. Historical Series No. 10. Philadelphia: Fortress Press, 1968.

________. *The Roots of Fundamentalism: British and American Millenarianism 1800-1930.* Chicago: The University of Chicago Press, 1968.

Schurmann, Franz. *Ideology and Organization in Communist China.* Enlarged ed. Berkeley: University of California Press, 1968.

Scofield, Rev. C.I., gen. ed., *The Scofield Reference Bible.* 2nd ed. New York: Oxford University Press, 1917.

Singh, Bakht. *God's Dwelling Place.* Bombay: Gospel Literature Service, 1957.

Smith, C. Ryder. *The Bible Doctrine of Grace.* London: The Epworth Press, 1956.

________. *The Bible Doctrine of Man.* London: The Epworth Press, 1951.

Smith, Daniel. *Bakht Singh of India: A Prophet of God.* Washington: International Students Press, n.d.

Sparks, Jack. *The Mind Benders.* New York: Thomas Nelson Publishers, 1976.

Stevenson, Herbert F., *Keswick's Authentic Voice.* Grand Rapids: Zondervan Publishing House, 1959.

________. , ed. *Keswick's Triumphal Voice.* Grand Rapids: Zondervan Publishing House, 1963.

Stewart, James Livingstone. *Chinese Culture and Christianity.* New York: Fleming H. Revell Co., 1926.

Stoeffler, F. Earnest. *German Pietism During the Eighteenth Century.* Leiden: E. J. Brill, 1973.

________. *The Rise of Evangelical Pietism.* Leiden: E.J. Brill, 1965.

Strachey, Ray. *Group Movements of the Past and Experiments in Guidance.* London: Faber & Faber, 1934.

Torrey, R.A. *The Holy Spirit: Who He Is and What He Does.* New York: Fleming H. Revell Co., 1927.

Tregear, J.R. *A Geography of China.* Chicago: Aldine Publishing Co., 1965.

Tse-Shing, Tang [pseud.]. *Death Blow to Corrupt Doctrines: A Plain Statement of Facts.* Shanghai: The Gentry and People, 1870.

Underhill, Evelyn. *The Life of the Spirit and the Life of Today.* New York: E. P. Dutton & Co., 1922.

Walvoord, John F. *The Rapture Question.* Grand Rapids: Zondervan Publishing House, 1964.

Wang, Mary. *Stephen the Chinese Pastor.* London: Hodder & Stoughton, 1973.

Warfield, Benjamin Breckinridge. *Perfectionism.* Edited by Samuel G. Craig. Philadelphia: The Presbyterian and Reformed Publishing Co. 1971.

Wehrle, Edmund S. *Britain, China and the Antimissionary Riots, 1891-1900.* Minneapolis: University of Minnesota Press, 1966.

Wesley, John. *Wesley's Standard Sermons.* 2 vols. Edited by Edward H. Sugden. Nashville: Lamar & Barton, n.d.

__________. *The Works of John Wesley.* 14 vols. Edited by Thomas Jackson. Reprint ed. Kansas City, Mo.: Nazarene Publishing House, n.d.

Yamamoto, J. Isamu. *The Puppet Master.* Downers Grove, Ill.: Inter-Varsity Press, 1977.

Other Sources Consulted

Adeney, David. "The China Watch." *Christianity Today* 20 (November 21, 1975):10-12.

American Board of Missions. *Foochow Missionaries Documents,* 1846-54, 1860-80, 1920-29.

Balsama, George. "Madame Guyon, Heterodox." *Church History* 42 (1973): 350-65.

Cheung, James Mo-Oi and Fredlund, A. Donald. "To Whom It May Concern." Letter, Christian Literature Crusade, April 19, 1973.

China Bulletin. 1949-1980.

Crane, Burton. "Evangelist Drive Sweeps Formosa." *New York Times,* October 8, 1950, sec. 1. p. 11.

Fritsch, Charles T. "Biblical Typology." *Bibliotheca Sacra* 104 (1947):87-100, 214-22.

__________. "To Anti-Typon" in *Studia Biblica et Semitica.* Wageningen, Netherlands: H. Veeman en Zonen N.K., 1966. pp. 100-111.

Gasque, Ward. "The Biblical View of Man." Cassette recording, Vancouver, B.C.: Logos Tapes of Canada, n.d.

Hollenweger, Walter J. "Unusual Methods of Evangelism in the Pentecostal Movement in China." *A Monthly Letter about Evangelism* 8/9 (November/December 1965):1-5.

Kaung, Stephen to Dana Roberts. November 13, 1972. Personal letter.

King, Harold G. "How I Kept Strong in Faith in a Chinese Communist Prison." *The Watchtower,* July 15, 1963, pp. 437-439.

The Stream. 1973-75.

" 'Little Flock' and Middle School Students." *Religious Education Fellowship, English Bulletin,* May 1937, pp. 33-34.

Lyall, Leslie. "Evangelization by Migration." *China's Millions* 58 (1950):170.

Markus, R.A. "Presuppositions of the Typological Approach to Scripture." In *The Communication of the Gospel in New Testament Times,* pp. 75-93, S.P.C.K. Theological Collections. London: S.P.C.K., 1961.

Murray, D.S. "The Building of the Church in Village Communities Twenty Years Experience in North China." *International Review of Missions* 7(1918):363-72.

Notson, Charles E. "Individualism Gone Astray: II. The 'Little Flock' of Watchman Ngnee." *The Alliance Weekly* November 12, 1952, pp. 729-30.

Pollock, John. "A Hundred Years of Keswick." *Christianity Today,* June 20, 1975, pp. 6-8.

Pryke, J. " 'Spirit' and 'Flesh' in the Qumran Documents and Some New Testament Texts." *Revue De Qumran* 5 (1965):345-60.

Rowley, H.H. "The Interpretation of the Song of Songs." *Journal of Theological Studies* 38 (1937):337-63.

Schmitt, Charles. *A Correction of the "Local Church Ground Teaching" as Held by Followers of Witness Lee.* Grand Rapids: Fellowship of Body of Christ, n.d. (pamphlet).

Spiritual Counterfeits Project. "Trip of the Month: Witness Lee and the Local Church." *Newsletter* 6 (July-August 1975).

Stearns, Mrs. Carol T. Church at Hollis, Hollis, New York. Interview, October 14, 1972.

Stuart, Douglas. Gordon—Conwell Theological Seminary, S. Hamilton, Mass. Interview, October 10, 1974.

_______. "The Bible, Dualism, and Christian Good Works." *Inside,* November 1972, pp. 18-22.

Stube, The Rev. Edwin to Dana Roberts February 16, 1975. Personal letter.

Dana Roberts was born on October 4, 1948 in Winchester, Massachusetts. After graduating from high school, he served in the United States Marine Corps as an electronics technician and a chaplain's assistant. In 1972 he received a Bachelor of Arts degree from Bridgewater State College, Bridgewater, Massachusetts. Four years later he was awarded a Master of Theological Studies from the New Testament Department at Gordon-Conwell Theological Seminary in South Hamilton, Massachusetts. In 1979 he received a Master of Arts in Religious Studies at Eastern Nazarene College for his research into the theology of Watchman Nee. Mr. Roberts is currently active in home missions for the Conservative Congregational Christian Conference and is a member of the Society of Biblical Literature.

In 1973, Mr. Roberts married Cynthia Wilcox of Easton, Massachusetts. They presently have two children: Jennifer and Rebecca.

For free information on how to receive
the international magazine

LOGOS JOURNAL

also Book Catalog

Write: Information - LOGOS JOURNAL CATALOG
Box 191
Plainfield, NJ 07061